THEY'RE NOT BOYS

SAFELY TRAINING
THE ADOLESCENT FEMALE ATHLETE™

by Warren J. Potash,
Specialist in Exercise Therapy and Sports Nutrition

*Dedicated to all female athletes that possess the spirit
to become the best each can be on and off their field of play,
and all of those who support their efforts.*

NOTICE

For educational purposes only. Every effort has been made to ensure that this information is as accurate and as timely as possible. Every user of this book can benefit from the authors' experiences in helping adolescent female athletes train to play their sports. This book should never be used for self-diagnosis of any medically related challenge. Only a qualified physician can address any or all medical challenges. Only use this book for informational purposes.

Printed in the United States of America
Publisher: LEARN2TRAINSAFELY.COM at www.learn2trainsafely.com
Printed by Createspace.com
First Printing: January, 2012
1 2 3 4 5 6 7 8 9 10

Author: Warren J. Potash, Specialist in Exercise Therapy and Sports Nutrition

They're not boys – safely training the adolescent female athlete™ ; Subtitle: All female athletes need to value training to play sports
by Warren J. Potash
Includes bibliographical references and an index
Preassigned: LCCN: TXu001727232
ISBN-13: 978-1461166146
ISBN-10: 1461166144

Table of Contents

Note from the Author. i

1. Youth Sports Programs for Teen Female Athletes 1

2. The Foundation Approach to Helping Adolescent Female Athletes 5

3. Helping Teen Female Athletes Now and into the Future 11

4. How Did We Get Here?. 19

5. Why Adolescent Female Athletes Need to Train to Play Sports 33

6. The Benefits of Female Sports Participation. 41

7. Coaching Today's Female Athlete 47

8. Training to Play Sports 65

9. Top Ten Reasons to First Focus on the Lower Body . . .79

10. What You Can Do to Help Your Daughter-Athlete .93

11. Nutrition for Daily Energy .109

12. Understanding Fundamental Training Concepts . . .113

Conclusion 127

Afterword 131

Appendix A: Sport Nutrition Guidelines 135

Appendix B: Challenges for Female Athletes at Puberty. . . .139

Appendix C: Concussions — Return to Play 141

Appendix D: The Responsible Use of Social Media 143

Appendix E: Researchers Conclusions about Females and ACL Injury 147

References and Websites Cited 155

Additional Resources – Reading and Websites 163

Index 165

Sports Participation and Injuries

Injuries are a possible part of any sports or recreational activity, or even during routine activities of daily living for everyone. Injuries cannot be totally prevented by this or any other training program. Warren Potash through Sport Fit Conditioning Programs and LEARN2TRAINSAFELY.COM provides general training programs to improve a person's fitness level and the sport-specific conditioning for young female athletes while minimizing their risk for injury.

The time-tested training guidelines improve the strength, power, speed, quickness, agility, flexibility and cardiovascular endurance for young female athletes. The risk of injury is not zero. Every athlete, her parents, guardians, coaches, and trainers must be aware of this fact.

A trainer can minimize the risk for injury for a female athlete by using the guidelines and progressions my colleagues and I have developed since 1995. A trainer can learn how to develop a safe and age-appropriate training program for female athletes. Information for these CEU courses are available at www.issaonline.com.

ACKNOWLEDGEMENTS

Special thanks to my wife, Millie, for her patience and for supporting all of my efforts during the additional hours I require to research, prepare, and spend training adolescent female athletes over the past 16 years.

To my colleagues, Stephen L. Gordon, Ph.D., and Bob Filer, MS, PT, CSCS. Your significant contributions produced our custom and sport-specific, functional/integrated training program that has helped more than six hundred adolescent female athletes since 1995. Your combined insight, experience, and expertise enabled us to develop a program that now has the potential to help minimize the risk, and hopefully reduce the numbers, of injuries for many more adolescent females in the years to come. I know the program's success is due to your knowledge and helping me develop safe and age-appropriate training guidelines and progressions for adolescent female athletes based on valued research.

Thanks to every researcher, and all health care professionals who work diligently to provide valuable insight so trainers and therapists can provide safe and age-appropriate training for all young female athletes in the field.

Dave Hagen, illustrator, has helped show that all female athletes need to have fun playing their sport and, at the same time, are serious athletes.

Devon Keefe Wible beautifully discusses what she experienced during her sporting career. This insight will help today's adolescent female athlete and all adults understand her sporting experience and how injuries can be minimized with safe and age-appropriate training. I also thank the young ladies who allowed me to share their experiences dealing with their knee challenges as adolescents.

Thanks to Coach Dawn Redd who provides her valuable insight about successfully communicating with young female athletes. I need to thank Karen Dolins, Ed.D. and Vicki Harber, Ph.D. for allowing me to use their excellent information that has been helping all female athletes. Louise Kelly, Ph.D., Professor of Pediatric Exercise Physiology at California Lutheran University (CLU), helped me by sharing her expertise with both this book and my website. Janie Rider, Ph.D., Assistant Professor of Exercise Science at CLU, provides valuable insight into the pre-Title IX world and what passage of this legislation has meant to her and her family.

Without Denny Adkins's help and guidance this book would not have been written. As the parent of two female athletes who played sports through high school and with his commitment to female sports endeavors; he always provides invaluable insight.

A special thanks to Charles Myers and the staff at the Atwood Library at Arcadia University for their help by providing much needed assistance in tracking down information when I was researching topics in Pennsylvania.

The Createspace.com team – many thanks for all of your help to best present this information.

I could rewrite parts of my website at www.learn2trainsafely.com and produce volumes of information. I do not see that as a benefit to educating adults about safely training their adolescent female athletes in this Internet age. Please realize there is a wealth of information from many researchers whose valuable work provides the foundation for every training program I use in the field. I have many more valued research titles and definitions of medically based words listed on the website.

Never look where you are going.
Always look where you want to go.
— Bob Ernst

Note from the author

Females are not males with less testosterone.
— Warren J. Potash

I coined this phrase many years ago. I always say that if you give me a chance to explain this statement, you will see that while females can become terrific athletes, their training must be different than that of males.

Sometimes, people want you to take them at their word. This is not what I am asking you to do to help your daughter-athlete. Give me a chance to offer you valued research that forms the foundation for the reasons why a statement is true. Take a look at why females need to train differently and learn what can be done to minimize their risk for injury♦.

Since 1995, I have trained more than six hundred adolescent female athletes in every sport. How have I been training young female athletes? Using guidelines developed by my colleagues based on valued research. Our approach builds a strong lower body from the bottom up in much the same way that a stable house must be built on a strong foundation.

Throughout this book you will notice that I am citing valued research from mainly 1990 forward; i.e., time-tested research that, just like my program, has produced a solid foundation for neuromuscular training for all participants.

I have attained remarkable results using our neuromuscular based training program. This type of training is now being recommended by researchers and all health care professionals as an integral part of stabilizing and strengthening the adolescent female athlete's lower body. I have helped every adolescent female athlete achieve, and/or surpass their initial hopes and dreams for their sport. As important to me is how this training has helped every youngster throughout their lives. Safe, age-appropriate, and integrated training helps every young lady succeed on and off their field of play♦.

I understand that some people just want information; don't confuse me with the evidence. Some of you will want to read the valued research abstracts or statements that supports the reason why teen female athletes need to train to play sports. I said that as a former Chemistry major, I know that a little catalyst can go a long way. I am asking everyone to now accept a sea change♦♦ – a transformation in thinking to help our youngsters stay healthy.

Other authors have written books about the environment that has caused the high non-contact ACL injury rate for female athletes. I am providing you with all of the relevant information, so you can make an informed decision about the female athlete's need to participate in neuromuscular training.

Finally, form your own conclusion about what is needed to provide safe and age-appropriate training for all teen female athletes. I know you will become a believer who is empowered with this quality information that can help turn around the current, too high injury rate for teen female athletes.

♦ No training program can guarantee an athlete will not suffer injury during training and/or their sports participation.

♦♦ Shakespeare (1611) coined the phrase when he wrote that a sea change is:

a seemingly magical change,
as brought about by the action of the sea.

There is nothing magical about neuromuscular training as it requires every female athlete to work hard and smart; but isn't life all about attaining goals when we challenge ourselves? The student-athlete appreciates the benefits from training to play sports and adults see her game rise to a higher level as she plays with more confidence.

Youth Sports Programs for Teen Female Athletes

You and your daughter have decided to have her participate in a youth sports program. Depending on her age and her ability – you will usually begin in a local program, and if she is really good – she may play in a club program.

You and your spouse may decide to become a volunteer coach &/ or work for the program to help with fundraising, bookkeeping, etc. Over time, your daughter has begun to transform into your daughter-athlete.

Now, adults in your program – the so called experts – are telling you what to do, how to do it, and letting you know that everything is being done with your daughter's best interests in mind. This is where I first step in.

I believe there are no adults that want to introduce anything that will harm a young female athlete. However, most of these adults – in fact the GREAT majority – may have played ball in school or college, or they have listened to other adults who began coaching a couple of years before and just did what they were told to do.

There are few youth sports programs that require an adult to gain certification to coach these youngsters. Matter of fact, when I suggested to a local youth group leader (some years back) for a park and recreation organization, that they should not allow youngsters to play unless the volunteer coaches were certified; the response was - we are afraid the adults will not do it and we will lose revenue if we tell them their teams are not able to play on our fields.

It is now time to reduce the too high rate of female sports injuries that have occurred over the past two decades. My interest in helping teen female athletes has always been to:

"minimize the adolescent female athlete's risk for injury so every female athlete can have FUN playing their sport(s)."

I have a very successful track record having trained female athletes since 1995 without any major injuries happening after the female athlete completed her training program.

Go to www.learn2trainsafely.com and read "About Us" and you will see that from day one – my only concern has been the safe and age-appropriate training for every female I worked with; matter of fact, this program has always been viewed as life skills training. This means we have offered integrated training for every athlete based on an initial assessment and Medical History to provide the safest training program for every female.

SKILLS TRAINING – this is what is valued. The next hurdle for all adolescent female athletes is to:

VALUE TRAINING to PLAY SPORTS.

There is no downside to safe and age-appropriate training to play sports!!!

> **FACT**: If a trained athlete is injured, she will return to play more quickly than an untrained athlete.

I WILL NOT JUST OFFER MY OPINION. In every instance, I will refer to valued research that forms the foundation for all recommendations.

Most adults who are volunteer coaches apply college age-appropriate training to young girls (if they train them to play sports) with open growth plate issues not realizing why this approach is wrong. Or, they believe that skills training is only what is needed. This is wrong!! If it were correct – then please explain the too high injury rate over the past 20 years.

Please take the time to understand all of the information I am presenting and at the end, you will believe what I know – there is a better way to help today's female student athlete. Let's put into practice training to play sports so the clouds from today's high injury rate gives way to a sunny tomorrow with less female athletes being injured; reducing the ACL injury rate over time that is so prevalent today in 2011.

When our daughter reached the age of sixteen or so, she joined a nationally recognized ASA softball team. Many of the girls were more "naturally" athletic than she, specifically with regards to running speed, and she realized it. We met Warren Potash at one of her games, found out about him, discussed our daughter, and believed he could help.

Our daughter began training with him for speed and fitness, and eventually the regimen adapted into improving her in all areas of softball. The improvements in her running speed and balance and overall dexterity were amazing. He transformed her into a young woman who was dramatically more athletic.

My wife and I would like to add that as happy as we were with the improvement in sports, we are more pleased about certain "life wisdoms" acquired from Warren Potash which over time have transcended the sports aspects of the training.

Our daughter attended college where she was awarded a Phi Beta Kappa Key and at present attends law school. She continues to work out and be aware of diet and fitness, much of which she learned from Warren Potash, and will probably do so throughout her life.

Warren Potash is an excellent athletic trainer, but more importantly, a person from whom a young woman can learn a great deal about the totality of life.

The Sodens
Proud and Pleased Potash Parents

Foundation Approach to Helping Adolescent Female Athletes

"What's the source and value of knowledge and the application of that knowledge to a particular subject in health science? I have discussed and dealt with this question for many years as a scientist and health science administrator. For nearly 20 years, I served as Chief of Musculoskeletal Diseases at the National Institutes of Health. This book considers a topic, athletic training for young female athletes, for which there is emerging new data, but most of that knowledge has not been applied to the subject population.

It has become overwhelmingly clear that young female athletes are not only injured as much as their male counterparts, but in many non-contact situations, their injuries are more prevalent. Yet the training for these young women is often deficient at best, or harmful at worst. There is enough available knowledge to make clear recommendations to improve this situation. Outlined in this [information] are some of the basic steps required for a safe, progressive program.

What is the source of the new information? As documented within this book, several articles in leading scientific journals have identified the magnitude of the problem and even provided some suggestions to improve specific components of a training regimen. Over the past years, I have applied the exercise principles established by Bob Filer and Stephen Gordon to prove that a complete, safe and rational program can be successfully delivered to young female athletes.

The approaches are based on current practices and recent research in physical therapy and sports exercise science. In applying existing knowledge to this young female population, it became quickly apparent that the only safe approach was to test the trainees regularly and build slowly before more advanced techniques could be delivered. This "new" approach is therefore based on current knowledge, common sense, and several years of program development.

What is the value of new information? There has been a huge increase in sports participation of young females over the past 20 years. The good news is that these participants gain many fitness and life-skill benefits associated with physical activity and organized petition. The bad news is that there has been an excessively high injury price paid for this participation. While complete elimination of injury is impossible to achieve, it is possible to reduce the injury rate. So the first valuable goal of this [information for online training programs] is to lower the risk of injury by having everyone understand that an adolescent female athlete should participate in an age-appropriate training program before playing her sport. The next valuable goal is for the training to translate into improved performance on the playing field. So far, every one of the participants have realized significant gains in speed, strength, endurance and/ or performance. As Warren Potash likes to say, "Each athlete becomes the best that she can be".

The final value considered within the principles defined in this book is that the young female athletes discussed are all student-athletes. That means that they need to integrate training and competition into a busy family, school, and social life. The Sport Fit Conditioning [Inc.] Program™ [licensor to LEARN-2TRAINSAFELY.COM] always considers the total person, not just the athlete."

— Stephen L. Gordon, Ph.D., 2003

WARREN POTASH COMMENT

Reading Dr. Gordon's words written almost eight years ago, I could ask him to write something new and these words and concepts would still be true today. I want all readers to understand that now – all parents, coaches, and trainers need to acknowledge that females must be trained differently than males. The parents need to expect that all of the volunteer coaches will create awareness for all young female athletes to value training to play sports.

With Dr. Gordon's template and Bob Filer's ability to apply valuable and safe progressions to safely train all females, we were able to develop guidelines that are standing the test of time and the most important test; they have worked for every adolescent female athlete who has trained with me. More than six hundred female athletes have benefited from this training program. This training program began as: Could we help these young female athletes? For me, there is no question as this training has now evolved to one-on-one or group training in the field and an at-home training program that can help every young female anywhere.

SIGNIFICANT INFORMATION

✓ Complete, safe and rational training program
✓ Foundation of all training is based on relevant and valued research
✓ Goals of LEARN2TRAINSAFELY.COM training program:
    o Lower the risk of injury
    o Translate into improved play
    o Integrated training program fits into student-athlete

Throughout this book, you will appreciate the female athlete's challenges at puberty and why using BNP♦ training to prepare to play sports is so important.

♦ BNP TRAINING

Balance, **n**euromuscular control, and **p**roprioception – the key to stabilizing and strengthening the knee joint allows an individual to optimally develop joint control when playing a sport.

Balance – The ability to keep one's equilibrium when varying forces are placed against the body; i.e., keeping one's center of gravity so she is ready to make sport-specific movements without compromising her lower body.

Neuromuscular control – The ability for the muscles surrounding a joint to support the internal structures of that joint to minimize the risk of injury. Power and balance are essential components for effective neuromuscular control and proprioception.

Proprioception – The ability for a body part to recruit the maximum signals to the brain to effectively control movement and body position to minimize that body part's risk for injury. E.g., the knee has two main mechanoreceptors for sending signals to the brain, the ACL [anterior cruciate ligament] and the PCL [posterior cruciate ligament]. By performing balancing with a flexed knee, the entire knee capsule's microtransmittors can be trained to also send messages quicker to the brain resulting in better control of the knee when running, jumping, and cutting.

– www.learn2trainsafely.com

When BNP Training [other quality training programs are available under different names] is completed, the teen female athlete can optimally control her body by lowering her center of gravity with efficient biomechanics that does not place excessive forces on the entire lower body. Specifically, the the ankles, knees, and hips are stabilized; minimizing the risk for injury and helping her become a better athlete.

"Warren Potash has trained all three of our children at one time or another. Each one of our kids is involved in a different sport. This means they each have different physical needs to accomplish the goals they are each working towards. Warren is very knowledgeable in sports specific training. Not only is he very good at knowing the best training techniques, but he takes the time to really get to know each person and is dedicated to helping them reach their goals. He is not only concerned about the outcome of his time spent in training athletes, but he is also concerned about the athlete as a whole. Warren is very knowledgeable and very committed to his work. He is awesome!!"

– K. & J. Connor

"Initially, I was skeptical about the sport-specific conditioning program that Warren Potash discussed with me and my daughter. As an RN, I knew that the type of program being discussed was not available anywhere else. Now, many years later and looking back at my daughter's career, I know the foundation she established when she was 14 to 15 years old helped her get to the next level of play during her softball career; especially the sports nutrition, mental toughness training, etc. that is part of the functional and integrated approach that is utilized by Warren Potash."

- T. Welsh, RN

HELPING TEEN FEMALE ATHLETES
NOW AND INTO THE FUTURE

I did not learn about Canadian Sports for Life [CS4L] and Vicki Harber, Ph.D., an exercise physiologist at the University of Alberta in Canada, until I had almost completed this book. Reading her research, it became apparent that we shared the same philosophy about helping female athletes. She says: "women are not men and children are not small adults."

I am describing her research since, like me, Dr. Harber presents valuable information about prevention for the short and long-term health of every female athlete. In this book, you will understand that it is not just Dr. Harber who says young female athletes need to train to play sports – it is all of the independent researchers who have reached this important conclusion that neuromuscular training will help all female athletes as part of an integrated training program. My training program since 1995 certainly validates what researchers have known for many years.

In May 2011, Dr. Harber published an important paper for CS4L: "The Female Athlete Perspective." She writes: "It is common for male training programs to be applied to females and adult training programs to be applied to children and adolescents. The assumption that the same training program will enhance performance in females, children, and adolescents limits athlete potential. Training programs are not a 'one size fits all.' Increased understanding about the uniqueness of the female athlete will lead to athlete-appropriate education, improved awareness and prevention of the conditions known to interfere with female athlete performance."

"Programs focusing on preseason conditioning, functional training, balance, core stability, education, and sport-specific skills are effective in reducing injury rates."

Many of these |musculoskeletal| injuries are preventable. Building awareness about appropriate support for young female athletes and changes to training programs are critical to help them reach their athletic and personal potential, injury-free.

The timing of these interventions is important. Prevention programs are recommended throughout the season with a special focus during the preseason."

She discusses the female athlete triad: "|it| urgently needs attention for young female athletes." She found: "attention must be paid to their proper nutrition to ensure both the athletic performance and healthy reproductive performance associated with bone health and overall well being."

She summarizes with: "**Implementing programs that address the unique needs of the female athlete will generate peak performances, but not at the expense of the long-term health of the athlete**."

Add Dr. Harber's information to what I have accomplished since 1995 with the understanding that more than six hundred teen female athletes have benefited from my integrated, sport-specific training program. Now, when healthcare professionals independently reach the same conclusion that female athletes need training programs that are developed for their unique medical challenges, it behooves all *adults, parents, and female athletes* to take notice. Sports participation for female athletes cannot be business as usual in the future.

Dr. Edward Wojtys |Voy ■ tus| says, "This |female ACL injury| is more than a sports medicine problem. It's becoming a public health problem." (**a**nterior **c**ruciate **l**igament* is one of the two knee ligaments – the other being the PCL; **p**osterior **c**ruciate **l**igament - both the ACL and PCL connect the upper and lower leg bones). (NY Times Sports; March, 2011)

Dr. Wojtys is a leading orthopedic surgeon and researcher helping female athletes and is the Director of the University of Michigan Sports Medicine Program. Doctors and trainers call female ACL injuries a "silent epidemic." Orthopedic surgeons have said they cannot believe the adult-like damage inside a young athlete who requires surgery for injuries historically seen in adults.

* Note: Ligaments connect bone to bone and tendons connect muscle to bone.

It does not have to be this way as there is a better way for female athletes to develop using safe and age-appropriate training by first

VALUING TRAINING TO PLAY SPORTS.

ABSTRACT - EXCERPT
High prevalence of knee osteoarthritis, pain, and functional limitations in female soccer players twelve years after anterior cruciate ligament injury.

OBJECTIVE:

To determine the prevalence of radiographic knee osteoarthritis (OA) as well as knee-related symptoms and functional limitations in female soccer players 12 years after an anterior cruciate ligament (ACL) injury.

Of the subjects answering the questionnaires, 63 (**75%**) reported having symptoms affecting their knee-related quality of life, and 28 (**42%**) were considered to have symptomatic radiographic knee OA. **Slightly more than 60%** of the players had undergone reconstructive surgery of the ACL.

CONCLUSION:

A very high prevalence of radiographic knee OA, pain, and functional limitations was observed in young women who sustained an ACL tear during soccer play 12 years earlier. **These findings constitute a strong rationale to direct increased efforts toward prevention and better treatment of knee injury.**

– Lohmander LS, et al. October 2004

Borrowing a phrase from Dr. Wojtys that I wholeheartedly agree with; female athletes should not expect a major injury as a result of their sports participation experience.

Yes, I am differentiating between females and males; mainly due to research that shows when a female injures a joint— more than 70 percent will develop osteoarthritis [OA] within twelve years, whereas males may develop OA in twenty years.

I do not want to see young women in their twenties or thirties suffering from soreness or pain for the rest of their lives and possibly requiring medication to alleviate the symptoms.

Obviously, no one can guarantee that injury will not occur when playing sports. But with the lower body stabilization and strengthening training programs now available, the young female athlete can place the odds on her side.

Females suffer non-contact ACL injury and this is much different than being hit or clipped [hit from behind]. We can minimize every female athlete's risk for non-contact ACL injury.

"This [female ACL injury] is more than a sports medicine problem," said Dr. Edward Wojtys, the Director of Sports Medicine at the University of Michigan. "It's becoming a public health problem."

– NY Times,

March 2011

MYTH — FEMALES DO NOT NEED TO TRAIN DIFFERENTLY THAN MALES

False! The female body is not exactly the same as the male's body. E.g., the pelvis is located towards the front of the body as compared to males. The differences bring a unique set of challenges for all females playing sports.

In Chapter 5, I present the many other challenges at puberty facing all female athletes.

There is no way to predict which youngster will develop into a D I candidate. It behooves all young females to train to play sports to minimize their risk for injury.

Look at what experts told the NY Times in March, 2011 about bio-mechanics and motor-development needs at the youth levels of female sport:

> One of the leading collegiate women's head basketball coaches was quoted as saying "girls are reinforcing poor biomechanical behavior by specializing in a sport too soon." As previously mentioned, but worth repeating is this quote from a leading researcher and orthopedic surgeon, Dr. Edward Wojtys who says "female ACL injury is becoming a public health problem." And a trainer at one of the top collegiate women's basketball programs says "If we want to turn this situation from an epidemic to something else, we really need to hit youth sports when they are in their motor-development phases. The habits they come in with are very difficult to change."

This book is written for adults and their daughter-athletes. Every reader can separate the truth about the benefits from training to play sports from the myths and the 'old time' thinking that are still being used.

Here is what some healthcare professionals have said:

> "The number of knee injuries among young female athletes has reached *epidemic proportions*," said Dr. James Elliott, an orthopedic surgeon at Ortho Montana, which is affiliated with St. Vincent Healthcare. "We are seeing players from all the high school soccer, volleyball and basketball teams. The injuries cut across every discipline."

"With year-round and multisport participation, many of our young athletes do not have time for recuperation, and injury potential increases dramatically," said Dr. Michael Willis, orthopedic surgeon at Billings Clinic. "Those injuries can be lessened through appropriate seasonal adaptation, adequate nutrition and by paying attention to signs and symptoms of overuse."

Dr. Peter Millett, an orthopedic surgeon and a partner at the internationally-renowned Steadman Clinic in Colorado, underscores Elliott's message, saying ACL tears in young women and adolescents are reaching "alarming numbers."

– The Billings Gazette website. November 2010

All of the evidence is alarming. One writer describes the female athlete knee challenge as 'reaching astronomical levels.' The key question is: what can we do to help our teen female athletes?

Now is the time for young female athletes to **VALUE TRAINING TO PLAY SPORTS**.

Play sports with a passion
but always maintain balance in your life.
– Sharon Backus, UCLA Softball

How Did We Get Here?

Prior to the enactment of Title IX, female high school basketball players played three-on-three on one side of the court; they could not run the length of the court. Six young ladies, not five, played in skirts; half on offense and half on defense. In my opinion, this is an example of limited opportunity for female athletes.

"Very often individuals recognize that discrepancies exist between societal expectations and their own personal values. As a result, role conflict is deemed to be present when a person perceives and/or experiences her or his role expectations as being incompatible" (Sage and Loudermilk. March 1979). Since sport has traditionally been considered as being more of a masculine activity, a female participant might perceive a conflict between her role as a female and that as an athlete.

"Combining the roles of woman and successful athlete was extremely difficult in American society until recently. Women wanting to be involved in competitive sports and continue to be 'feminine' were confronted with social isolation and ridicule. By selecting a physically active life, women were disassociating themselves from traditional female gender-role expectations. Women athletes failed to fit the ideal of femininity, and those who persisted in sport activities suffered as a result" (Barry CH. 2008). A traditional perspective of female participation in sport has been summarized by the statement: "Sports may be good for people, but they are considered a lot gooder for male people than for female people" (Gilbert and Williamson, 1973).

"Female student-athletes generally experienced more role conflict than male student athletes." (Lance LM. 2004)

HOW TITLE IX SHAPED TODAY'S SPORTS PARTICIPATION

Prior to 1972, there was limited opportunity for a female student-athlete to play sports in high school and college. Look at how far we have come from this quote:

"No person in the United States shall, on the basis of sex, be excluded from participation in, be denied the benefits of, or be subject to discrimination under any programs or activity receiving federal financial assistance."

— From the preamble to Title IX of the Education Amendments of 1972.

Title IX is a section of the Educational Amendments passed by Congress in 1972. This legislation prohibits discrimination against girls and women in federally funded education, including athletic programs. Soon after Title IX passed, the NCAA and high school administrators complained that boy's sports would suffer if women's sports became equally funded. Additional regulations were later released and they were implemented in July 1975.

Enforcement of Title IX came to a halt under Presidents Reagan and Bush. The 1984 decision, Grove City v. Bell, the U.S. Supreme Court gutted Title IX saying that it did not cover entire educational institutions, only those that received federal funding. Four years later Congress passed the Civil Rights Restoration Act of 1988; this canceled the effects of the Grove City ruling.

This law has led to the many opportunities that female student-athletes enjoy today. Unfortunately, it has also led to many male sports being dropped in the name of equality. I doubt the founders of this movement anticipated that sports would be cut across the country due to gender-equity considerations. Administrators still struggle with the equality rules from the enactment of Title IX.

FEMALES JUST PLAY SPORTS

ATHLETICISM defined:
1. Of or befitting athletics or athletes.
2. Characterized by or involving physical activity or exertion; active: an athletic lifestyle; an athletic child.
3. Physically strong and well-developed; muscular…"

– http://www.thefreedictionary.com

I am hoping, in the future, we can add to this definition that the majority of adolescent female athletes immerses herself to understand and appreciate the fine points of her sport and trains her body to play sports.

PLAYING A SPORT – When female (or male) athletes just play one sport from an early age and do not use their muscles differently, the vast majority of them will not be as athletic as those who have developed sound muscle memory by having to respond differently when playing different sports; in effect – cross training their body and using their brain in different ways to enhance their motor abilities. Playing different sports helps them best develop motor control and athleticism.

We are in an era with much research showing that a vast majority of female athletes participate in sports for social reasons primarily, and are not immersed in their sport. More importantly, we are developing student-athletes who just play their sport rather than developing athletic females who ooze athleticism and then, after trying different sports in childhood, choose one that matches their strengths.

THE MORE ATHLETIC A FEMALE ATHLETE BECOMES, THE MORE FUN SHE HAS PLAYING HER CHOSEN SPORT WHILE MINIMIZING HER RISK FOR INJURY; BY PREPARING HER BODY FOR THE RIGORS OF HER SPORT

For example, female tennis players are nowhere to be found in the USTA Top 10 professionally (if the Williams sisters had not been injured recently, they would be ranked in the Top 10). Watching matches, it is apparent that many of the American players are not as "athletic" as foreigners.

They can hit the ball, but their court awareness and ability to mentally sustain their optimal effort is challenged by their opponents over time. Why is this? At a young age, moms and dads are dropping off their daughters to hit the ball, often in group lessons. Their ability to immerse themselves in the game suffers.

Therefore, when they reach college age and older, they do not have the background to play tennis at the very highest level. The best may have personal goals, as a pro, to make money and be ranked between numbers 11 and 25, or higher in the world which is a fine goal for those extremely talented young women. But this will not allow these female athletes to consistently compete for major championships.

One of the knocks about a vast majority of female athletes is they do not hang around their sport to study it and really learn its ins and outs. When they are not playing, they are not watching others play in person or on the television or computer. They are off to do other things.

They are not training to get ready to accept the demands of their sport. Since it is a fact that a majority of young female athletes play sports for social reasons. Today's parents and youngsters do not realize that training to play sports is the next challenge for all female athletes to learn, appreciate, and perform.

For example, a softball player has to throw a softball overhead. Even though a smaller ball is used in early years, wouldn't it be easier to teach the proper 90/90 overhead throwing motion if the female athlete's rotator cuff and upper body was prepared prior to doing all the throws that youth coaches demand of their athletes?

The same can be said about directional kicking in soccer, the serve and kill in volleyball, or the three-point shot in basketball. In all instances, developing the body leads to better muscle memory for perfecting technique. It is very difficult to change three or four years of incorrectly kicking, throwing or serving, and shooting a ball if musculoskeletal challenges are present.

I think you get the idea. Correctly trained muscle memory prepares the body for the demands of the game that the athlete chooses. By playing different sports, or with safe and age-appropriate training – the female athlete can enhance her experience as she has prepared her body properly.

Valuing training to play a sport takes a commitment that is not for everyone. There are leaders and there are followers. It takes all kinds to make this world go round. Please do not think I am saying that every teen female athlete must become a serious athlete. However, I do believe that since every female athlete should want to challenge herself athletically - if for no other reason than to minimize her risk for injury - she needs to do so by stabilizing and strengthening her joints to prepare her body to play sports.

Training and playing as I describe would help decrease the current, too high injury rate and help all female athletes become more athletic; they'll be better balanced and better able to react quickly with faster movements in all directions. Every trained female athlete will become:

FASTER, QUICKER, MORE AGILE, and STRONGER and develop lean muscle.

The adult volunteer coaches, parents, and trainers have to emphasize this BNP Training [other quality training programs may have a different name for this core and lower body neuromuscular training] as a development that is integral to every young female athlete's participation requirement to play sports. The following was said many years ago (it is just as relevant today) by Dr. Edward Wojtys:

"There is no doubt that there are neuromuscular differences between males and females. Depending on their sex, athletes fire different muscles for the same task. Women also tend to run, jump, and land in a more upright position than men."

"Women shouldn't accept ACL injuries as the price they have to pay for being athletic."

I say that it is time for all adults and their daughter-athletes to value training to play sports so all female athletes can have fun playing their sports. No one can have fun if they suffer a major injury, as you will read about later in this book from interviews of two injured adolescent female athletes..

HEALTH CARE PROFESSIONALS HAVE KNOWN FOR YEARS

In March 2004, a consensus statement |was| released by a collaboration of associations that outlines several musculoskeletal and medical issues specific to female athletes and the related implications for prevention and care. The document, intended as a guide for team physicians, was developed by the American Orthopaedic Society for Sports Medicine, American Academy of Orthopaedic Surgeons, American Academy of Family Physicians, American College of Sports Medicine, American Medical Society for Sports Medicine, and American Osteopathic Academy of Sports Medicine.

John A. Bergfeld, M.D., at the Cleveland Clinic and a member of the consensus panel, said |in 2004| the statement represents "fresh new data based on good research, not just personal opinion." He said the real value of the consensus statement would be increased awareness about the gender-specific issues related to female athletes.

"We are trying to increase awareness that there is a little bit more to think about with female athletes," he said.

Edward J. Wojtys, M.D., editor of *Orthopedics Today's* Sports Medicine section, said that it **"has become clear that the female athlete is different from the male athlete**. Nutrition, training, health issues all need to be addressed in a gender-specific manner and recent research have supported that. In the past, **training of female athletes was conducted the same as for male athletes. That clearly was not the right approach**."

– Holliman K. Orthopedics Today. March 2004

LISTENING TO WHAT FEMALE ATHLETES SAY
Title IX was the beginning of the growth in female sports participation as we know it today. I present valued research in the benefits section from a researcher that describes Title IX as the 'lightning rod for the explosion of female athlete sports participation' that has come after 1972.

Therefore, every reader should read what a student-athlete who attended Princeton University has to say about her training to play softball (and other sports) through high school and college and what she experienced playing softball at Princeton University. This young woman recently married and her words today are as true as when she wrote them after graduation from Princeton University.

I believe that what young women have to say about training to play sports is the ultimate test as to whether today's female athlete should consider training as integral to playing sports in conjunction with their sport skills development. Female athletes who are trained in a safe and age-appropriate manner after going through a male type training program cannot believe it is possible to make significant gains without their body being beaten up. They know they are working hard. They never realized that smart training for female athletes is different than the training for males.

However hard and smart for a female recognizes the inherent differences at puberty and helps them become strong and develop more power while looking good when they are dressed up or at the beach; i.e., lean muscle is valued for the 99.9% of the female athletes I have trained.

Would anyone reading this book say they would rather see a female athlete go to a physical therapist for rehab after a major injury? The injury may require surgery and significant loss of time playing their sport.

Read what Bob Filer, one of the best sports medicine physical therapists in the Philadelphia, PA region and primarily responsible for the guidelines used by Warren Potash since 1995, has to say later on. I think you will agree with his statements.

Quite simply:

EVERY ADOLESCENT FEMALE ATHLETE CAN GREATLY BENEFIT FROM TRAINING TO PLAY SPORTS.

There are many trainers who do not appreciate the significant differences between the sexes and still use a male training format for the female athletes they train. Hopefully, in the years ahead, trainers who have not completely thought through how to safely train teen female athletes will either take our CEU courses [since 2003; I do not know of similar courses that are currently available] at www.issaonline.com, and/or better understand how to provide safe and age-appropriate training programs for all females who want to minimize their risk for injury and become a better athlete.

MYTH – MY DAUGHTER-ATHLETE WILL GET AN ATHLETIC SCHOLARSHIP TO PLAY SPORTS IN COLLEGE

The myth that early specialization in a single sport will help a youngster obtain an athletic scholarship to play her sport in college has resulted in an athlete who plays one sport from an early age. Adults believe this is the only way.

This is not true! An athlete (in 2011) who earns an athletic scholarship receives four one-year renewable rewards, not one scholarship for four years. It is renewable from the college or university based on criteria for the student-athletes at each institution.

There are adults who prey on a parents' belief that a scholarship is the carrot that all young athletes should chase. Please do not be naive about how many adults earn their livelihoods on the backs of today's youth. These individuals have a vested stake in having adults spending their money to help their daughter-athlete succeed. Few athletes trickle through and earn scholarships.

Every year, maybe several thousand young women are fortunate to earn full or partial scholarships. When these youngsters started out, there were many millions of females playing sports. I have seen stats that show as few as 1.45 percent of all females earn (partial or full) scholarships to play sports in college. More scholarship money is awarded for academics than athletic prowess at NCAA schools. The latest statistics show that $1 billion was awarded in athletic scholar-ships as compared to $20 billion for academics.

For example, a D I university has sixteen sports for women. The NCAA mandates so many scholarships for each sport. Let's say there are eighty full-time equivalent scholarships available for all teams. So, maybe one hundred or so females can get a full or partial scholarship. What are the odds your daughter will get one of the five for basketball? How about one of the scholarships in soccer? Even if all NCAA schools offered this many athletic scholarships, approximately 0.75 percent (not the 1.45 percent I have seen) of all female athletes will get a shot at a full or partial D I scholarship each year. Not great odds.

There are nearly five thousand colleges in the United States and they all offer academic scholarships. Solid academics and playing sports through the teen years provide many more opportunities than just being a good athlete. Multi-tasking and strategic thinking skills are valued by all employers. The female with a solid foundation to think quickly on her feet while being able to consider all of her available options will do very well during, and after her playing days have ended.

If your daughter is a student-athlete, playing sports may help her get into the school of higher education she wants to attend - if she continues her athletic career. Further, if she is considering a Divi-sion III (there are no athletic scholarships for D III schools) school, she could obtain more academic money from the school than if she was not an athlete. My own daughter fell into this category. She graduated in the top 15 percent of an excellent academically ranked high school and received far more in academic scholarships from that institution when she decided to play basketball and softball in college.

The power for our teen female athletes choices lies within the family unit; the adults and the student-athlete making choices. If building certain values has taken a back seat to all sports all the time, take a step back and breathe deeply and figure out what your family needs to do. If your daughter's studies have taken a backseat, now is the time to have her buckle down and get her priorities in order.

You say the coach of your travel team is not happy. If this is true, what are the real motives of the coach and that organization? Do they really care about your child? Or, is it about winning or losing games? Is the organization losing some money because you dare to allow your daughter-athlete to play another sport with a different organization? Maybe a decision is reached to not attend their summer camp and you are told she must participate if she wants to play in the fall.

I have six-week, nine-week, and thirteen-week training programs. The thirteen-week program produces optimal results, but limited playing during this training is frowned on by travel coaches. Researchers today are trying to determine the minimum time a female athlete needs to train. I hope that everyone understands that time off is good for females so they can rest their minds and prepare their bodies for the rigors of competition and practice. But athletes cannot expect to accomplish as many gains in six or nine weeks of training as compared to a thirteen week program.

So, let's be real! It was reported by the travel industry that just youth sports travel, et al spending today is $7 billion annually (all youth sports). That does not include the fees each team pays to participate in tournaments. I am certain that youth sports will continue to be the one sport variety from an early age and repetitive-motion type injuries will continue. Therefore, the information in this book explains what needs to be done to combat what is the teen female athlete's reality, and what can be done to help our youngsters since the one sport type challenges for female athletes will most likely continue to occur for the foreseeable future.

DID YOU KNOW? In many foreign countries, youngsters do not play sports to win or lose. In fact, winning and losing is not a factor until youngsters are about fourteen years of age.

The emphasis is about skills and training their body for the demands of the sport. E.g., in soccer, youngsters play three-on-three or seven-on-seven games that teach them to react quickly, make precise passes, and really learn the geometry (angles) of playing and understanding the nuances of soccer.

College coaches are seeking female athletes who are athletic. They are seeking those athletes who are skilled and smart to provide flexibility for the coach as the collegiate student-athlete's sports participation is much different than their travel club days. An exception; skill players like a pitcher in softball.

The coaches value youngsters who will mature into low maintenance athletes and team-first oriented student-athletes.

Why Adolescent Female Athletes Need to Train to Play Sports

The vast majority of adults and adolescent female athletes do not value training to play their sports. Females face many challenges at puberty that same-age male do not encounter.

EVIDENCE-BASED RESEARCH

There is an unacceptably high injury rate for the female athlete, primarily due to non-contact anterior cruciate ligament injuries. These ACL injuries happen at a rate as much as three to nine times higher than male athletes (Gillette Children's Specialty Healthcare, December 3, 2010; research cited). Researchers have determined there are many reasons why female athletes are more prone to ACL injuries, including biomechanical, physiological, hormonal, and cognitive issues. Researchers say the reasons are complex and connected to the following:

- Absence of neuromuscular spurt at puberty (as compared to males).
- Female triad — osteoporosis, eating disorders, and amenorrhea (loss of period).

- Wider hip to knee ratio ("Q angle") and pelvis is anterior (to the front) as compared to a male pelvis being towards the posterior (to the back).
- Jumping using quads and landing hard.
- Running upright.
- Possible hormonal changes.
- Muscular imbalances and weaknesses.
- Quadriceps dominance [quad is the muscle in the front of the upper leg].
- Lax (loose) joints; i.e., properties of ligaments and tendons.
- Playing sports without training.
- Growth plate and joint development.
- Lack of coordination and fatigue.
- CNS [central nervous system] – Cognitive - Female Injury

Dr. Frank Noyes, a leading researcher and orthopedic surgeon, also explains some of these differences. "To withstand the twists and turns for aggressive sports, hamstring muscles should be 60% to 70% as strong as the quadriceps. In female athletes, the ratio is 45% to 55%."

My experience for untrained athletes has been 38% to 41% ratio, reaching 45% to 50% after thirteen weeks of training. Dr. Noyes continues: "Also, females rely on their quadriceps when jumping and running (pivoting), while males depend more on their hamstrings. Since the hamstring muscles are more protective of the ACL, that muscular imbalance is considered a risk factor in knee injuries."

Evidence-based research shows that adolescent female athletes should not be trained in the same manner as same-age male athletes. The female's body is not ready to play and "the many repetitive motions may cause injury, especially when there is a lack of training prior to sports competition" (Hewett T, Noyes F. 1996).

Researchers are seeking programs that take into account the evidence affecting the adolescent female athlete; i.e., a program that is safe and age-appropriate and one that will provide a strong foundation for every adolescent female athlete.

The good news is that female athletes can train in a foundation program to minimize their risk for injury. The bad news is that not enough females are doing so, and the amount of teen female lower-body injuries — specifically the non-contact ACL injuries — are still at historical highs when compared to same-age males [three to nine time higher rates for female athletes as compared to same-age male athletes].

In 1999, Dr. Mary Ireland described the "position of no return" (i.e., where the middle of the knee tracks in front, or to the side, of the toes). Female athletes can be trained to minimize these vulnerable positions. By avoiding these positions, less force is impacting the knee joint. This is the primary reason that females suffer **non-contact ACL injuries**; i.e., the knee "blows out" when increased forces affect the joint over time.

Parents and coaches need to understand there is no downside to safe and age-appropriate training for teen female student-athletes. Since no training program and no coach or trainer can guarantee that sports participation will not result in injuries, please understand that a trained athlete will return to play faster than an untrained athlete.

True champions aren't always the ones that win,
but those with the most guts.

– Mia Hamm, American Soccer Pro

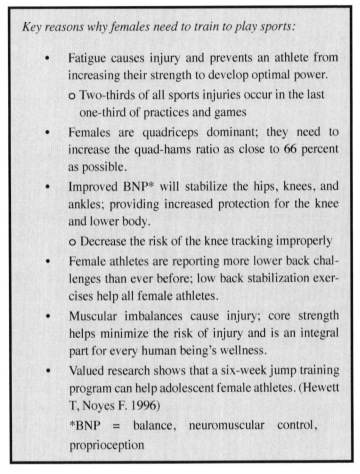

Key reasons why females need to train to play sports:

- Fatigue causes injury and prevents an athlete from increasing their strength to develop optimal power.
  o Two-thirds of all sports injuries occur in the last one-third of practices and games
- Females are quadriceps dominant; they need to increase the quad-hams ratio as close to 66 percent as possible.
- Improved BNP* will stabilize the hips, knees, and ankles; providing increased protection for the knee and lower body.
  o Decrease the risk of the knee tracking improperly
- Female athletes are reporting more lower back challenges than ever before; low back stabilization exercises help all female athletes.
- Muscular imbalances cause injury; core strength helps minimize the risk of injury and is an integral part for every human being's wellness.
- Valued research shows that a six-week jump training program can help adolescent female athletes. (Hewett T, Noyes F. 1996)

  *BNP = balance, neuromuscular control, proprioception

WHAT DOES WARREN POTASH MEAN BY "FEMALES ARE NOT MALES WITH LESS TESTOSTERONE"?

Adolescent and adult female athletes require a solid program that incorporates all of the key elements of training. A trainer must first look at any unique challenges found in a medical history and a baseline assessment. With this information, the trainer prepares exercises so the athlete can participate in a safe and age-appropriate training program.

Many untrained females will not bend from the knees or jump and land with soft knees. Why is this so? The challenges at puberty do not allow the female's body to work efficiently. But the good news is these inherent challenges can be minimized with proper training to play sports.

There is no way around it – boys and girls have significant differences at puberty. These differences need to be accepted so that proper and safe exercises are utilized to help young female athletes stay healthy.

For example, some coaches punish athletes for their mistakes with extra push-ups. While I do not agree with this approach, a better method for females would be to have them perform some stomach crunches or train their core with other exercises. This is because females have inherent weaknesses in their shoulders and upper back and push-ups can hurt them with a limited number of reps [repetitions].

GOAL: Coaches and trainers of female athletes must appreciate the female's physiological and biomechanical challenges, and understand how to use safe and age-appropriate training techniques to implement the teen female athlete's training program. <u>Additional female athletes changes at puberty</u> (other than the challenges at puberty previously noted):

- Size of heart, volume of cardiac stroke (beats per minute) and size of left ventricle are smaller.
- Lung volume and aerobic capacity are less.

- Hemoglobin levels are reduced.
- Female is smaller and has shoulders that are more narrow and reduced articular [bone] surface.
- Female has greater flexibility and increased balance.
- The process of puberty in females impedes their best sports performance by lowering their physical optimum.

– Greydanus DE, et al. 2010

RESEARCHERS ROLE IN HELPING FEMALE ATHLETES

Since the passage of Title IX in 1972 (as I previously noted) more and more females are playing sports. While there is no doubt that the passage of this legislation was the beginning of this growth, does this explain why females are injured with greater frequency than males?

"There is no doubt that there are neuromuscular differences between males and females. Depending on their sex, athletes fire different muscles for the same task. Women also tend to run, jump, and land in a more upright position than men...

Women shouldn't accept ACL injuries as the price they have to pay for being athletic." (Wojtys EM., et al. 1996)

Researchers dive into the complexities of the female athlete's many challenges to determine what should be done to help them. As an orthopedic surgeon, I am certain that Dr. Wojtys has seen far too many female athletes with ACL and other knee injuries through the years. Since he is a leading researcher, his research offers valuable perspective about this challenge.

What does the female athlete need to embrace?

TRAINING TO PLAY SPORTS is the next hurdle for the teen female athlete to learn about and understand its significance for two reasons:

1. Stabilize the lower body — use BNP training; i.e., balance, neuromuscular control, and proprioception (see www. learn2trainsafely.com).

2. Becoming faster, quicker, more agile, and stronger to develop more power while minimizing the risk for injury allows every female athlete to play with confidence and to become the best she can be on and off their field of play when combining BNP and core training.

It is estimated that between seven and one-half to almost ten million girls are playing sports today through age eighteen. With all that is known about how important safe and age-appropriate training is for all adolescent female athletes, it is time for today's female athlete to minimize her risk for injury with a BNP training program.

BNP training (and other quality training programs) has the potential to make a major impact by minimizing the risk for the ACL type injury. How can that be? By allowing for optimal function of the lower body combined with core stability:

"Core Stability...provides a stable base to allow optimal kinetic chain function. Optimal function – |a| weak core does not allow for production of efficient movements leading to possible injury" (Ireland M, M.D., et al. 2002)

"Most teen female athletes ACL and other knee injuries are non-contact. No one clips or hits the athlete. The knee just gives out. Generally, the knee goes past the "position of no return." Dr. Mary Ireland defines this as when "the knee goes beyond the toes, inside, outside, or over the front placing additional and significant forces on the entire knee joint" (1999 Journal of Athletic Training article previously cited).

Paraphrasing Tim Hewett, Ph.D.: safely train your female athlete. She will become a better athlete.

"An ACL injury for a female athlete doesn't just affect them at the moment of injury; a high percentage of female athletes who suffer an ACL injury experience long-term consequences such as osteoarthritis and disability. This is unacceptable."

– Zebis MK, Ph.D. 2009.

"To tailor the most effective training regimen for the female athlete, it is important to consider sex-specific susceptibilities to injury. By exploring the biomechanical, neuromuscular, and cellular mechanisms of injury risk, it is possible to develop and implement appropriate preventive and treatment options tailored specifically to the female population."

– Groeger M. 2010

"Existing evidence points to a combination of therapeutic interventions including balance, strength, and neuromuscular coordination = Reduction in ACL injury."

"Female athletes have a 3–9 times greater risk of non-contact ACL injuries than males [research cited]."

"One in ten high school athletes will suffer an ACL injury."

– Matheson JT, et al. 2010

The Benefits of Female Sports Participation

The health benefits of increased physical activity and sports participation opportunities for female athletes can be traced back to Title
IX [being] responsible for much of the growth in women's athletics
and has also served as the lightning rod for much of the controversy
surrounding the impact of the same growth" (Carpenter LJ, Acosta
V, 2008) A few of the most important benefits females enjoy are:

- Physical activity can reduce a woman's weight and risk of
  developing cancer and other diseases. (National Women's
  Law Center. 2004)
- Girls who participate in some kind of sport experience
  higher than average levels of self-esteem and lower levels
  of depression. (Colton, M. & Gore, S. 1991).
- Sports participation is associated with reduced rates of
  body dissatisfaction and eating disorders (Tiggemann M.
  2001)

The behavioral benefits of increased physical activity and participation opportunities are:

- Female athletes have better grades and higher graduation
  rates than non-athlete females. In high school, athletic
  participation can lead to college scholarships. (National
  Women's Law Center. 2004)
- Seventy-one percent of female students who entered
  NCAA Division I programs on athletic scholarships in 1998

graduated within six years of enrollment, as compared to 63 percent for female students overall. (NCAA, 2005.)

- Young women who participated in sports were more likely to be engaged in volunteering, be registered to vote, feel comfortable making a public statement, follow the news, and boycott more than young women who had not participated in sports. (Lopez MH & Moore K. 2006)

- Teenage female athletes are less likely to use illicit drugs, less likely to be suicidal, less likely to smoke, and more likely to have positive body images than female non-athletes. (Miller K, et al. 2000)

- Team sports participation is associated with a lower prevalence of sexual risk-taking behaviors for young women. (Kulig K, Brener N, McManus T 2003)

- Female athletes are less than half as likely to get pregnant as female non-athletes (5 percent and 11 percent respectively), more likely to report that they have never had sexual intercourse than female non-athletes (54 percent and 41 percent respectively), and more likely to experience their first sexual intercourse later in adolescence than female non-athletes. (Women's Sports Foundation. 1998)
  – http://www.aauw.org/act/laf/library/athleticStatistics.cfm

- Female athletes having greater opportunities to play sports leads to greater female participation in previously male-dominated occupations, particularly for high-skill occupations. (Stevenson B, 2008)

ADDITIONAL BENEFITS

If you were asked to draw a classroom, most people would sketch a room with four walls and a variety of desk configurations. Few would sketch a swimming pool, tennis court, ball field, ice arena, ski slope, or basketball court. Yet the lessons learned in these unconventional classrooms are rarely taught anywhere else. My colleagues and I developed an integrated, sport-specific training program so each young woman will learn about daily and sports nutrition, strategic thinking skills, proper goal setting, time management skills, and mental toughness between the lines. This is training that helps them now and in the future.

Why is sports participation important? For the same reasons more traditional academic subjects like science and math or participating in marching band, etc. are important; athletics develops skills and opportunities young people need to excel in life. Here are some specific outcomes from the female athlete's participation in athletics:

- A report from the Feminist Majority Foundation's Task Force on Women and Girls in Sports cited a study showing that women who exercise regularly significantly reduce their risk of contracting premenopausal breast cancer — by as much as 50 percent. That study parallels findings of a 1981 study conducted by Dr. Rose Frisch at Harvard's Graduate School of Public Health, which showed that young women who participated in college sports, or who exercised regularly in college, were significantly less likely to contract breast cancer and other reproductive cancers.
- Other physical benefits of athletic participation, documented by a large body of research, include increased cardiovascular endurance and strength, which decreases the chances of heart attacks, strokes, back problems, osteoporosis, and other health problems.
- The Institute for Athletics and Education reports that high school girls who play sports are 80 percent less likely to be involved in an unwanted pregnancy, 92 percent are less likely to be involved with drugs, and three times more likely to graduate from high school.

- A study by Melpomene Institute, a women's health and fitness research organization, found that girls derived positive self-esteem from sports through challenge, achievement, risk-taking and skill development.

Athletic participation helps girls learn about goal-setting, pursuing excellence in performance, and other achievement-oriented behaviors — all critical skills needed for success in later life. Deb Erickson, a personal development trainer who has worked with women's athletic teams, says that, in her experience, she's found that girls and women who participate in athletics have a more highly developed sense of personal power, freedom, and autonomy.

"In sports, there is an explosion of energy that gives women and girls a chance to experience voice and power and position," Erickson said. "Girls can perform in band or choir and learn about cooperation and teamwork, but they don't get the physical release and bonding that comes from sports.

"Sports help women reclaim their own personal sense of power and control in their lives. Athletes have confidence and inner strength and are in tune with their own energy and power."

> – http://www.essortment.com/all/psychologyofsp_rdhl.htm

It must be noted that studies have shown that females who play sports share the following traits (www.kidshealth.org):

"Sports and exercise are part of a balanced, healthy lifestyle. People who play sports are

- Healthier,
- Get better grades,

- Are less likely to experience depression,
- And use alcohol, cigarettes, and drugs less frequently than people who aren't athletes."

The Women's Sports Foundation has listed the top 25 benefits for females playing sports at:
http://www.womenssportsfoundation.org.

"Sport participation [for females] is great for building confidence and self-esteem while decreasing levels of depression. In addition, sport participation provides a means to build important life skills, such as teamwork and goal-setting, while having fun and staying in shape.... There are also important health benefits obtained from participating in sports and physical activity.... Sport participation is also an important component to building strong bones, which will decrease the risk of osteoporosis as they age."

– American College of Sports Medicine

COACHING TODAY'S FEMALE ATHLETE

In the long run, the value of sports has little to do with running,
jumping, or throwing. The ultimate merit is in teaching females to
appreciate battle and males to value bonding. At its best,
sport teaches us how to be whole people and thereby,
prepares us for a more successful life.
– Kathy DeBoer

A NAVIGATIONAL MAP FOR COACHING FEMALE ATHLETES
by Coach Dawn Redd, www.coachdawnwrites.com

I don't know the profile of the typical person who will read this book. Maybe you're a mom or dad who wants to make sure that your daughter achieves all that she is capable of during her athletic career. Or maybe you're a coach who has never coached female athletes before — and you've heard lots of horror stories about working with girls. Or you could be an athletic trainer looking for an additional tool to add to your rehab tool belt. Whatever your job in life, I'm sure you're reading this book because there are female athletes in your life that you care about.

I can tell you, without a doubt, that coaching female athletes has been the joy of my life. I've spent almost twenty years in women's athletics. I played volleyball at the University of Wisconsin and have coached at the club, middle and high school, collegiate Division I and III levels. Female athletes are fierce competitors, hard workers, and amazing teammates when they are coached properly. So let's begin with the end in mind, as Franklin Covey says, and talk about our ideal female athlete — and then how a coach can go about creating that person.

PROFILE OF THE IDEAL FEMALE ATHLETE

When I think about the qualities of the great athletes that I've coached in the past, they have a combination of eight wonderful characteristics that are summed up in the list that follows. These traits will be a starting point for the rest of this chapter on coaching female athletes. I believe that we can have both high expectations and high standards for our players, but I also believe that successful athletes don't just happen — it takes a coach to guide them.

 Before you coach your first snap or serve or kick, you've got to know what success will look like to you — when will you be happy with the outcome of your athletes? With that in mind, I came up with a list of traits that I think that successful and motivated female athletes should carry:

Confidence. The confident female athlete has confidence in herself, her abilities, and the future of the team. Confidence is essential to any sort of success your team may have — and it's got to be consistent. Situational confidence is based on a specific performance and is short-lived, to be crushed by the next loss or poor performance. But genuine confidence? Now that's the good stuff! It is a belief the athlete holds deep down within herself that she will ultimately be successful.

Success. Successful athletes are hard workers, focused, diligent — willing to sacrifice their time and energy on a goal. These athletes are always striving for more. Whether it's the non-starter who becomes a starter, or the starter who makes all-conference, or the all-conference player that receives national recognition — success is often the result of a lot of sweat equity put in by the athlete.

Self-motivation. In my mind, this is the best trait of them all! Every drill, every game, every weight room workout is only as good as the amount of effort our athletes are willing to put in. For those athletes who are internally motivated to work hard in the off-season, during preseason, in the weight room — those are the athletes who will see tremendous improvement over the course of their careers.

Hard work. There's only one person who knows if your players are working to their full potential and that's the players themselves! We can put them into physically and mentally challenging situations in practice, but it's up to them to truly challenge themselves. We all hope that we've got a team full of players that will never "dog it" in a drill or not push themselves in a practice, but in the end, it comes down to the athletes themselves. Those players who are willing to keep their foot on the gas pedal throughout the entire season will ultimately experience success.

Leadership. The responsibility of being a team leader is exciting to some and daunting to others. There's always debate about the vocal leader versus the leader by example and about which is better. While it's rare to find both of those qualities within one athlete, leadership can be taught. An openness and desire to lead is essential because I don't think that you can thrust leadership onto someone, but rather it must be accepted.

Teaminess. That's a word that I've made up to describe the state of an individual who values their teammates and enjoys being in a team environment. The "teamy" player puts their teammates first and is willing to sacrifice personal glory for the good of the team. Teaminess occurs when a group of people come together with a common goal, a common purpose, and a common level of dedication.

Skill. Being skilled at a sport takes time and effort and repetition. It takes a desire to not only execute in practice, but to perform each movement correctly. Why is skill so important? Because all of the intangibles in the world won't do the team much good if it's not combined with skill. But when those intangibles are combined with skill, the player should be motivated to work at their sport with a laser-like focus.

Hunger. I'm sure we've all coached the athlete who was blessed with a tremendous heaping of skill, only to throw it away through laziness. I'm not talking about that athlete, but rather the one who is skilled and willing to work to better their already finely tuned skills. The athlete who wants to win and be successful so badly that they can literally taste it. The player who is being propelled by a desire to get better every single day.

Now that we know what our successful female athlete looks like, let's look at what we can do, as coaches, to get them to that place.

CREATE TEAM CHEMISTRY

We can't leave team chemistry to chance, we've got to actively pursue and promote chemistry among our athletes. In an article I wrote for Athletic Management magazine, ("Women Warriors," October/ November 2010), I talked about how "even your best and competitive female athletes want to fit in and have a sense of belonging." If that's the case, and I believe it is, then it's even more important for coaches to put in the work of creating great team chemistry — and it starts at the top. Here are five steps you can take to be on your way to awesome chemistry among yourself and your team.

Be human and approachable. As the coach, you are the leader of your team, that's a given. But you have to be sure to maintain your level of approachability and openness. Always remember that you've got the upper hand of power in your relationship with your team, therefore it's your job to build the bridge of rapport. Ask them how their day at school was. Or if you know they've got a tough test coming up, be sure to mention to them that you know they're going to ace it.

Care about them. Your athletes want to believe that you care for them as people — not just for the particular grouping of skills that they have. Spend time talking to them about their classes or their parents or whatever. I've got a young lady on my team who loves the TV show *Glee*, and we've been able to bond over our mutual love of the show.

Have them over to your house. Break out of the monotony of the gym or the field and bring them over to your house for dinner. Not only will they get to see your other side, they'll appreciate time to hang with you without "talking shop" being the goal. It's a powerful thing for them to see the other side of "coach." They probably understand, in theory, that you have other interests in your life besides coaching them. This could be your chance to become a little more human to them.

Support them in things that aren't a direct benefit to you. Do you have players who are in the orchestra or who dance or who are involved in student government? Whatever it is, surely they have interests in things that don't involve you. Ask them about it! Attend whatever correlating functions go along with their activity. That way, when you tell them that you care about them, they'll actually believe you. Imagine how amazing your player would feel if you got the entire team together to watch their concert. Can't you almost feel the chemistry forming?

Ask them what they think. We coaches think we know it all, don't we? I know I do. I've never even met you, and I know that you think you're always right. You've probably got a mix of personalities on your team and the one thing that they have in common is that they probably think they're right too. Some of your players are bossy and love the opportunity to give their opinion. Others are quiet ruminators and won't give their opinions unless asked. But when you do, you'll be amazed at the depth of their opinions. Either way, taking the time to ask will be noted and appreciated.

Working on team chemistry should be the first order of business. In the early weeks of my season, I actually build it right into my practice plans. Sometimes our team chemistry activity will be a silly game and sometimes it will be a section of practice devoted to learning more about each player. I'm a firm believer in forcing chemistry early in the season so that it's more natural when it really counts.

FIGHT "GIRL DRAMA"

From the emails I receive on my Coach Dawn Writes blog, "girl drama" is the problem that most frustrates coaches of female athletes. If I could have a cause as a coach, it would be to eliminate the world of this perception that female athletes can't get along.

You may be thinking, *Well, Dawn, you coach collegiate athletes, but my middle school girls are ripping each other apart!* I've coached middle and high school as well as at the Division I and III collegiate levels, and I've learned one major lesson: *the coach sets the tone*. It's our job as the coach to understand what makes female teams tick and what motivates each athlete.

As Kathy DeBoer says in her book, *Gender and Competition: How Men and Women Approach Work and Play Differently*, "Until recently, it was not politically correct to think of women as different. If you said women were equal, then they couldn't be different. The wonderful news is we can now say women are equal and different. And that's a huge and dramatic breakthrough." So now that we know it's legitimate to say that female athletes are different than male athletes, let's cut to the crux of the issue.

The coach runs the show. Do you secretly believe that females are "catty" or can't get along? Then that'll come across to your team. How? You'll let bad behavior slide because you think that it's somehow a female trait. If two people have a conflict and they're men, it's no big deal. But if they're women, they're catty.

So the first thing is to evaluate your belief system and make sure that your team understands what you will and will not accept. I'm pretty explicit with my team about this whole "girls can't get along" thing and how I think it's a crock. The next step is to empower them with conflict-resolution skills.

At the heart of the matter, "girl drama" is just two folks (or a group of folks) who won't talk to each other about a disagreement they've had. The drama comes in when the rest of the people on your team are forced to pick sides in the fight. I'm sure you can see that the easy fix is to let them know that it's okay to have a disagreement — and it's also okay to go to the person with whom you're having a disagreement so that it can be discussed.

I certainly don't expect my team to make it through an entire season and not have issues that need to be addressed, but I haven't given them license to brush it under the rug of "girl problems." Conflict doesn't have gender and, as coaches, we can't give our teams excuses to not learn how to effectively deal with those conflicts.

TRAIN LEADERS AND FOLLOWERS

The beautiful part about coaching athletes of any gender is the life skills we get to develop within them — leadership being essential. When dealing with female athletes, it's a generally held belief that girls are raised to cooperate and boys are raised to compete. Knowing that, teaching our teams how to lead (and how to follow!) is critical to their development as athletes and people. Because girls are cooperation-based, the coach will have to take steps to protect their captains and other team leaders from being seen as separating from the group.

In my time as a coach, I've had girls who dreaded being voted captain because they didn't want their teammates to think that they were "stuck up" with their new position. I've also had players who refused to listen to their captains because "she thinks she's better than me."

Taking time to define leadership for the entire team, not just your team leaders, will help everyone be on the same page and fight any girl drama that wants to sprout up because of the stratification among players.

Here are the five qualities I think any good captain or team leader must possess. Going over all of these with your entire team will let your leaders know what they should be doing and show your followers what they should expect from their captains. *Integrity: Who are they when no one is looking?* A great team leader will be *committed* to working out in the off-season, hosting recruits, and being a good example for the rest of the team. They have a sense of *humility* about them, never wanting to abuse their perceived power position. They hold themselves and their teammates *accountable* to a high standard of excellence in the classroom as well as on the field or in the gym. They are *motivated* to portray a positive image of the student athlete: hard working, active on campus, and involved in the classroom. Finally, they are *prepared*. They know the scouting report, they come in early to help with whatever the coach or team needs, and they let the coach know of any problems that may be brewing in the background.

Awareness: Are they willing to be who their teammates need them to be? There's been a shift in the business world from following the Golden Rule (Do unto others as you'd have them do unto you) to the Platinum Rule, which says that we should do unto others as they would like to be done unto. The thought is that doing what I want could very possibly be exactly opposite of what you want, and therefore the bridge isn't passed. The good leader knows their teammates well and how they communicate.

Inspiring: Can they help focus the team on the common goal? When your captains sit down with the team at the beginning of the season, they should be the folks who are actively submitting ideas for those goals. They have (hopefully) been thinking about this for a while and have a vision that is as big as the coach's and encompasses the whole team.

Straightforward: Will they squash small issues before they become major drama? I'm sure all of us coaches meet with our captains regularly. And I'm sure that most of us ask them about things that are going on behind the scenes that we should know about. The straightforward leader will have noticed any issues that were rearing their ugly heads, respectfully gone to that teammate, and will have gotten it taken care of before we even know to ask.

Confident: Can they rally the troops in good times and bad? Being a team leader is a tough job! We require them to be the vocal leader as well as to lead by example. We ask them to commit to working hard toward an unseen goal. And we ask them to keep their teammates motivated even when their classes are killing them, the team has just lost a big game, or the pressure's on because you've won a lot games in a row.

Building these qualities into our team leaders is a time-consuming job — but well worth it in the end.

CREATE A COMPETITIVE CULTURE

I'm sure you've heard folks complain that female athletes aren't as competitive as their male counterparts. This is usually uttered by the exasperated coach of a female team. But as DeBoer says in her book, "properly motivated women are just as competitive as properly motivated men. The difference is the motivation, not the competitiveness."

Consider this scenario: It's game point in a close volleyball match. The two teams are pretty evenly matched. They've been trading points the whole game. Your team is about to serve for the game and the opposing coach calls a time out. You huddle your team close around you and you look your server in the eye intensely and tell her, "It all comes down to you, Susie — we won't win without you!" You think you're firing her up and showing her that you believe in her. She hears: "Don't screw up! If you miss this serve, your team will hate you!"

Women are very competitive and will rise to any occasion — together. Studies show that women get onto teams to be a part of something and to socialize, *then* once they realize that they're good, they'll keep playing. That's exactly the opposite of guys who join teams because they're good and happen to make friends along the way. So, the moral of the story is, if you want to motivate your female athletes to greatness, remind them of their teaminess.

At that same time out, bring your team in, huddle them up close and (while making eye contact with all of them) say: "Ladies, you all have worked your tails off to get to this point. You've hit, you've passed, you've set, you've played amazing defense. Now, Susie is going to crush this serve and we're going to win this game."

You've said the same thing as the first example, but now you've included her in a group effort.

SET GOALS

One of my favorite quotations about teams and about goal setting says that, "You must never confuse faith that you will prevail in the end — which you can never afford to lose — with the discipline to confront the most brutal facts of your current reality, whatever they might be."

Goal setting should not be a one-time thing at the beginning of the season. Whether they're individual or corporate goals, the coaches and the team should take time to re-evaluate where those goals stand.

The quote above is from James Stockdale, a man who was able to embrace both optimism and realism (a great trait for any coach to have!) in an amazing way — as a prisoner of war in Vietnam. While our situations most certainly are not that severe, we do have an obligation to look at our teams with that same mix of optimistic realism. Let's look at three areas where the discipline to confront reality is necessary:

Revisit team goals. When your team first got together, they sat down and wrote out some team goals that they thought they'd be able to accomplish by the end of the season. They showed them to you with pride. Maybe they even posted them in the locker room. At the halfway point of your season, it's time to check in on those goals. Have you already accomplished some of them? Then push your team to create bigger and more difficult goals. Or do you need to tweak those goals because you're no longer able to accomplish them? Regardless of which side you fall on, make sure that your team's goals are serving their purpose: to motivate them and push them to greater heights.

Evaluate midway performance. Every practice should involve evaluation, but the halfway point should bring with it a new eye to your non-starters. Are they getting better? Would you feel comfortable putting them in the game at any point? Are they still motivated (and trying to get some court time) or have they resigned themselves to being on the bench? In terms of your starters, who are your gamers? Who do you want in control at crunch time? How about your offensive and defensive scheme? Is it working the way you'd planned or do you need to change it up? These are all good questions to ask yourself at the halfway point.

Take stock. How's the team's morale? Are they fired up and motivated? Are they a tight-knit group who enjoy each other's company and operate like a well-oiled machine? The halfway point is also the time to review your coaching plan. Do you know how each of your players is motivated? Are you doing that? Is there anything that you can do differently to ensure that your players continue to improve through the end of the season? Finally, recruiting. When you take an honest look at your team, what are you missing? Can those holes be filled through your recruiting efforts? If so, you'd better get after it!

By re-evaluating your goals, you'll be more able to push your athletes individually and to motivate them as a team, encouraging them to continually work hard and challenge each other in practice. Having attainable goals gives each member of your team a reason to step into the gym or onto the field every day.

SUMMARY

I love coaching female athletes, and I'm not being sarcastic! I love that girls and women care about each other on a deeper level than just teammates. I love that female athletes believe in the power of team. But most of all, I enjoy showing my female athletes that women can get along — and that they can have fun, and battle, and be successful together.

This doesn't just happen, though. You've got to be intentional about creating an atmosphere in which your female athletes can thrive. Remember the traits of our ideal female athlete from the beginning of the chapter? Wouldn't we all be happy if our athletes were confident, self-motivated, successful, hard-working leaders? And wouldn't we be ecstatic if our teams were full of teamy players who were skilled and hungry to get better?

Well, your team can be just like that if you put the time into not only teaching your female athletes the X's and O's — but also the intangibles.

Creating amazing team chemistry, fighting "girl drama," training your leaders and followers, setting attainable goals, and tying it all together by creating a competitive culture are five solid ways that we, as coaches of female athletes, can make their athletic experience something amazing.

NOTE: This article by Coach Dawn Redd provides valuable insight for parents, coaches, and trainers of female athletes. Dawn's website, www.coachdawnwrites.com provides other valuable resources.

I believe the following quote sums up what every coach must strive to do:

> "My responsibility is getting all my players playing for the name on the front of the jersey, not the one on the back."

– Unknown-

MORE INSIGHT FOR COACHES

Joan Steidinger, Ph.D., discusses coaching female athletes:

"Ken Grace, who I worked with for several years, currently coaches younger athletes at Chabot Community College in Hayward, CA. He sums up that coaching young women is much easier than young men for the following reasons:

- Girls listen and boys challenge when it comes to coaching and teaching a new concept.
- Girls generally underrate their athletic ability and their ability to be competitive, and boys (at least at the community college level) think they are better than they actually are.

- It is easier to create a team atmosphere with a group of young women as opposed to young men. Men tend to create a ranking system quicker with each knowing their place on the ladder.
- It is extremely important when coaching young athletes, especially girls, that the coach focuses on positive aspects of every workout.

Steidinger continues that "as a sports psychologist, I've found **teaching young female athletes the basic mental skills of sports helps provide them with a basic foundation of discipline, focus, strength, and commitment**."

What is participation in sports teaching adolescent female athletes?

One would think that with 8U national tournaments stressing winning that winning is most important. But, there is so much more for our youngsters to learn. The following quotes stress attitude and goal-setting and the focus required to meet and surpass those goals:

A person's attitude, effort, and commitment provide the power and passion that make unique and special things happen.

– Jill Sterklel, University of Texas women's swimming

Once realistic goals are set, met, and surpassed, the female athlete is empowered to perform at a level that was previously unattainable. So, now the female athlete will want to be surrounded by like-minded females who share common values. Independent and strategic thinking skills can now be honed and then, this quote sums up what separates the women from the young ladies:

It's important that people know what you stand for — and what you won't stand for.

– Mary H. Waldrip

As the student-athlete's career ends, sports participation is now a metaphor for what every successful young woman needs to attain for what she hopes to accomplish in her lifetime. So what is sports participation teaching? Life skills training. Generally, the athlete only realizes this as she gets older and gains perspective on what happened along the way.

Joan Steidinger, PhD, also writes:

"Adolescent girls and athletics are a powerful force. Sport participation allows girls to physically and mentally stretch their limits. Sports teach girls about basic life skills. Basic life skills developed by sports include:

- Learning to establish goals and objectives,
- Practicing positive thought habits,
- Learning to develop motivation,
- Focus and concentration skills,
- Building confidence about training and abilities."

Therefore, every female athlete who tries her best is a winner in this game of life. As a trainer of young women, watching this transformation many times over, I am very pleased to have played a role in helping these young ladies be the best each can become.

The athlete's spirit carries that individual through life's challenges. As former NFL All League quarterback and coach Norm Van Brocklin said, "An athlete's greatest glory lies not in never falling, but in rising every time (s)he falls."

I never imagined as a thirty-something that I would face challenges for which no one could prepare me and my family. But what I learned from playing very competitive basketball from youth leagues to high school, college, and to semi-pro provided a foundation of perseverance that allowed me to see the light at the end of the tunnel with this challenge. We never gave up.

Jim Valvano, head coach at North Carolina State and master motivator, showed this never-say-die attitude as he met a cancer challenge head on. "Never give up" was his closing whenever he spoke. Since his untimely passing, his fellow coaches have kept his dream alive to beat cancer by raising many millions of dollars; determined to find a cure by fulfilling his attitude.

Time and again, you can ask a former athlete and he or she will tell you the same thing: "I got more out of sports that I could have imagined." Trying your best will follow you through every moment in your life and leads to a fulfilling career, no matter what one chooses to do.

Set high goals, and be positive so others who share
your goals will work together to attain them.
– Jody Conradt, University of Texas women's basketball

I have always used the adolescent female athlete's training as an opportunity to integrate all essential topics they require to help them appreciate and understand how to be successful on and off their field of play:

- ✓ Proper goal setting*,
- ✓ Increased strategic thinking skills,
- ✓ Mental toughness training - focus between the lines,
- ✓ Sports vision training – sometimes referring to doctor for glasses,
- ✓ Nutrition for daily energy, and
- ✓ Time management skills.

* Proper goal setting: the goal must be attainable by the individual. E.g., I want to bat 50 points higher than last year or I want my foul shooting percentage to be 85%. These are goals that the athlete can achieve.

I want to be the MVP or make the All-Star team. These are not examples of proper goals as the athlete cannot make it happen – it is out of her control; coaches gather in a room and vote about these selections.

*"When I go out on the ice, I just think about my skating.
I forget it is a competition."*
– Katarina Witt

Training to Play Sports

Smart and age-appropriate training helps make the knee joint stronger by first training the ligaments and tendons (in the joint) and the surrounding muscles. This provides the best way for the signals to move as quickly as possible between the knee and the brain for lightning quick adjustments. In other words, microneurotransmittors under the patella (knee cap) are trained to operate with optimal function as messages are relayed faster and faster as the training progresses, so adjustments can be made in a split second.

Look at what a fifteen-year-old experienced after having a history of ankle sprains and being out for several weeks many times over before I trained her. These are her own words:

> "As a high school freshman I was unsure of what exactly I was accomplishing from this fitness program, and I had voiced it to Mr. Potash. It wasn't until I was warming up before a softball game that I truly understood.
>
> I had experienced ankle problems in the past, and Warren and I had made a conscious effort to strengthen not only my ankles, but all of the muscles surrounding and supporting them. As I was doing "karaoke" I stepped into a hole in the ground and I felt my ankle wanting to twist. I dreaded the thought of being unable to play ball for a month just because of my weak ankles. However, much to my surprise I was able to correct myself and my body movement to

completely avoid the injury all together. I was absolutely shocked, but finally it made sense why I had been waking up at five in the morning to train three to four days a week.

All of the balancing, core training, plyometrics, stretching, sprints and hard work had paid off because I was able to prevent an injury just because of proper training. Aside from avoiding injury, I can honestly say that from this program I was in the very best shape of my life both mentally and physically. The emphasis on mental toughness has had a lasting effect on my life, and is something that has guided me through adversity to obtain my goals.

My strength grew tremendously and I saw a significant increase in speed as well as [in] my overall softball game."

– Emily M

I have seen what Emily describes many, many times. However, the more significant challenge we are presented with is to lower the too high non-contact ACL injury rate for adolescent females playing sports.

This table indicates risk factors for ankle sprain. Training the young woman's lower body from the bottom up♦ will positively affect certain risk factors indicated in the following table.

"Non-Modifiable Risk Factors	Modifiable Risk factors
Sex	Weight
Age	Body Mass Index (BMI)
Height	Bracing/Taping
Race	Footwear
Foot/Ankle Anatomy	Neuromuscular Control
Extremity Alignment	Postural Stability
Previous Ankle Sprain	Muscle Strength
Generalized Joint Laxity	Exposure to Sport
	Player Position
	Playing Surface
	Skill Level

Neuromuscular control/postural stability"

Looking at the risk factors in this table, you must note that BNP Training can also be very effective with some of the Modifiable Risk Factors:

- ➢ Neuromuscular Control
- ➢ Postural Stability
- ➢ Muscle Strength
- ➢ Exposure to Sport

Previous ankle sprains can be positively affected with BNP Training.

"Proprioception and broader neuromuscular control were first proposed as a risk factor for ankle sprain by Freeman et al in 1965. Subsequent studies have extensively and rigorously evaluated proprioceptive deficits after primary ankle sprain and described their resultant effects on strength, postural balance, and ankle stability, particularly in athletic populations."

– CPT Waterman BR, M.D., et al. April 2011

✦ A <u>distal</u> [furthest away from top] <u>to proximal</u> [closest to top] <u>approach</u> is used with all BNP Training to establish a solid foundation for every female athlete who participates in neuromuscular training.

WHAT DO TEEN FEMALE ATHLETES NEED TO DO?

Some people think the discrepancy in injury rates between female and male teen athletes is solely because there are more female athletes playing today. So, of course, female injury rates are higher. These people could not be more wrong!

When the apple-to-apple comparison is made in every sport, females are up to nine times more likely to injure their ACL than same-age males. Basketball, soccer, and volleyball (with field hockey and lacrosse) are the leading sports; These are fast-twitch dominant (there are fast, intermediate, and slow twitch muscle fibers) sports that feature cutting on a dime, stopping quickly, jumping and accelerating often with a cutting maneuver. In addition, as young women get stronger, the physical nature of each sport takes its toll on female athletes who are not in the best of shape and have not trained to stay away from the *position of no return*.

In 1999, Dr. Mary Ireland [in Sports Medicine Update] explains this topic:

"There are obvious static differences in anatomy in the female compared to the male. The more important factors in ACL injuries are movement patterns, the way the athlete moves, jumps, lands, and cuts.... ACL tears captured by videotape in basketball allow us to see this high risk position; more upright, hip internally rotating, and knee in valgus |e.g., knock kneed athletes|.

Anatomically, the female has a wider pelvis, increased femoral anteversion |a turning forward|, valgus knee, externally rotated tibia and prorated |e.g., flat footed| foot. Comparing the sexes, the position and control of the trunk, low back, and pelvis are different. The female has an anteriorly |front| tilted pelvis, greater lumbar lordosis |inward curve of the spine|, and subsequently greater hip internal rotation and adduction |inward|. This pre-existing position allows a more awkward landing from which the athlete cannot recover. This is the "**position of no return**" ... |that causes non-contact ACL injury|.

The |training| program |for female athletes| would include balance, strengthening, and position awareness. **Get more flexed. Get down!** ...

We must now go into the prevention arena.... Physical movement classes should occur very early in life, teaching children to land safely and in control, similar to the cry of "get down, stay down" routinely heard during youth soccer. Similarly, strength training programs can address landing as well as foot movements during cutting in basketball. Coaches should issue stern warnings when athletes demonstrate a high-risk movement pattern such as one-leg landings, out of control baseline landings, or straight leg landings. The warnings may serve to keep the athlete from "touching the hot stove again" for fear of getting burned."

Dr. Ireland concluded her research more than ten years ago, but it takes time for theory to work itself into the mainstream of female athlete training. Fifteen years ago, Tim Hewett, Ph.D. and Dr. Frank Noyes showed how effective a six week jump training program is for adolescent female athletes. And, since 1995 the female athletes I have trained have had remarkable success using our proprietary training program to help more than 600 teen female athletes.

In 2009, Gretchen Reynolds reported for the *New York Times* that "according to the results (Hewett, et al, 2009) young women whose ACLs had popped exhibited more trunk sway than the men or the uninjured women; when they landed, or planted a knee to switch directions, their upper bodies wobbled to one side. This placed great pressure on their planted knee, collapsing it inward and overloading the ACL. "Our research suggests that the issue in injured female athletes," Hewett says, "is a lack of high-level ability to control deceleration and acceleration at the center of their mass in three-dimensional space."

In other words, *they don't adequately steady their upper bodies as they move*. "Typically, he says, the problem blossoms in puberty. "Prepubescent athletes move alike, boys and girls," Hewett says. But then, although maturing girls sprout in height, they add comparatively little strength, unlike boys. "Their center of mass moves higher and they add weight, but not the power to control it," he says. They've primed themselves for knee damage."

Happily, if Hewett's theory holds, athletes can train away some of that risk. Specific exercise programs that target strength and balance or proprioceptive deficiencies could "reduce female athletes' risks until they're almost comparable" to the risks for male athletes, Hewett says."

Keeping a low center of gravity with proper biomechanics keeps the middle of the knee over the first and second toes when cutting, jumping and landing softly, running, and sprinting. This minimizes the risk of injury and helps every trained female athlete become faster, quicker, more agile, and stronger.

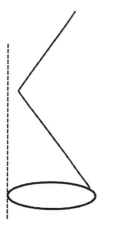

Side view – knee vs toes

> **"Position of No Return" MUST be Avoided**
> All lower body training must develop an awareness of where the knee is versus the toes with proper tracking.
>
> The knee can never go beyond the toes; i.e., middle of knee tracks between 1st and 2nd toes to minimize the risk for injury.

MYTH – IT COSTS A LOT OF MONEY TO TRAIN

False. At www.learn2trainsafely.com the at-home BNP Training Program is very cost effective (price is subject to change). This includes all of the equipment every female athlete requires to participate in this foundation program.

Considering that the average adult whose daughter plays travel sports or club sports is spending far in excess of several thousands of dollars per year, this program is something that just about everyone can afford. The athlete must be cleared by her physician to train to play sports before she begins; even with at-home training.

WHAT NEEDS TO BE DONE?
When possible, all female athletes will benefit from a training program to play sports that is safe and age-appropriate and conducted with a qualified trainer who understands the challenges that teen female athletes face.

This program consists of a:

- Medical history
    o Proper consent forms prior to first training session
- Baseline assessment
- Training program developed for teen females
    o Warm-up (increases blood temperature)
    o Stretching
        ▪ Hold all stretches 12-15 seconds♦
    o Strengthening
        ▪ Core strength program
            • Features low back stabilization/strengthening; i.e., spine-safe training
        ▪ Obliques [sides of torso] included
        ▪ Trunk rotation included
    o Cardiovascular
        ▪ Interval training
            • No advanced or plyometric training until sufficient leg strength
        ▪ Pool, if available – running in deep water
    o Cool-down

✦ It takes a minimum of 12 – 15 seconds for the stretch reflex signals to go back and forth from the body part to the brain; i.e., for the muscle to be stretched optimally. The maximum would be 30 seconds.

> Note: If there's a referral from a doctor or physical therapist, a report should be sent every four to six weeks to the healthcare professional.

I have developed challenging programs that are based on a strong and stable foundation for every female: BNP — balance, neuromuscular control, and proprioception. It does not have to be costly to train. At-home programs will benefit the teen female athletes who cannot work with a qualified trainer.

At-home training is certainly better than not doing any neuromuscular and core training. However, training with a qualified trainer during one-on-one or group training will help a female athlete perform every exercise in an optimal manner; i.e., every repetition needs to isolate the body part being stretched or strengthened.

Whether training at home or with a trainer, every athlete requires the discipline to follow the directions and perform every rep with precision to gain the maximum benefit when isolating each body part:

Practice makes Perfect, Perfect takes Practice, & Practice makes Permanent.

It is my hope that as more and more volunteer coaches find out how beneficial BNP training is, they will insist on a neuromuscular-based dynamic warm-up before practices and games and utilize BNP and core training as integral to the female athlete's development.

SPECIFIC PARTS OF A SUCCESSFUL CONDITIONING PROGRAM FOR FEMALE ATHLETES

One area that must be addressed is safe and age appropriate training. Since the advent of the one sport athlete in the past twenty plus years, repetitive motion type injuries are out of control. If there is going to be the one sport athlete, then cross training principles must be used at the younger and adolescent levels.

Clearly, one goal must be for athletes to have **FUN** while learning skills – skill development without the pressure to win is another goal. By using challenging and fun exercises, the coaches must learn how to integrate cross training into their practice routines.

> Note: I have had the athletes play dodge ball. Using a frisbee and playing seven players to a side for two hand touch. Running side by side and catching a ball between two athletes (or more) to see who can run the fastest without dropping the ball. Anything a coach can think of that challenges the youngsters and lets them have fun when training.

Stretching – there are no studies for stretching that state that if you start something in youth it will continue. But common sense says that, like anything else, if proper stretches were taught at young ages, these techniques will develop into habits that will carry over to the teen and adult years.

Also, coaches want repetitions for skill development and will sacrifice warm-up, stretching and cool-downs. We have to teach youngsters the proper way to warm-up and stretch (includes stretching at home and making certain that all body parts are stretched several times through each week), not just having a brief warm-up with a few second hold and call it stretching. E.g., 3-way calf stretches should be taught along with the achilles and soleus stretches and proper quad, hamstring, and IT band [the iliotibial band is located outside of the upper leg and tightness contributes to knee injuries] stretches for the legs (not performing all stretches at every session). The athlete must concentrate to perform every stretch correctly.

Females are generally more lax [looser] than males. They do not have the shoulder strength that males have. Therefore, in throwing sports, proper training and proper biomechanics are required for the female athlete to attain the 90/90 throwing position. Special running, cutting, and jump training should be taught to young female athletes to account for anatomical differences between the sexes, with emphasis on proper recruitment of muscles and correct body positions when executing each movement. They must land softly with flexed knees [not hard on their heels] when jumping, and powering off of the foot when running; these are just two examples of this type of training.

Teen and all female athletes require:

- Custom training program – baseline testing and information from a Medical History, etc. is used to develop an individualized program for each athlete – minimize weaknesses over time.
- Age appropriate – expectations from trainers and coaches for athletic performance.
- Age and gender appropriate training – stretching, strengthening, and cardiovascular endurance, as well as muscle endurance.
- Sport-specific – functional/integrated training; at a minimum sports nutrition for the female athlete should be part of the program.

- Cross training principles – incorporated into training.
- Stretching – 12 to 15 second holds, minimum, with proper biomechanics.
- Balance, Neuromuscular training, and Proprioception [BNP] with flexed knee and balancing in many different positions on flat and hard to balance surfaces; e.g., using half round Styrofoam.
- Proper biomechanics – throwing, hitting, jumping, running, kicking, etc.
- Running, cutting, and jumping – teaching proper recruitment of muscles and landing and all movement positions to enhance muscle memory and motor abilities while minimizing the risk for future injury.
- Mental toughness training – how to focus in sport(s) during training and games and letting it go afterwards without beating up one's psyche.
- Sports Nutrition – teaching females how to make certain they have enough energy to train and play sports, as well as all other important activities including proper rest and sleep.
- FUN – through all age levels teaching how to balance the desire to win with the enjoyment of participation.

FEMALES AND SPORTS PARTICIPATION

Sports is training for life skills. Just like other opportunities – marching band, performing arts, etc. Therefore, the expectation must be for having all participants have fun and feeling good about themselves after properly learning new skills.

In helping young ladies to the next level, health must become a priority. No more having colleges receive athletes all banged up before they get there. Each female athlete's health must be the top priority.

"Gutting it up" must be reexamined so that females are not playing through injuries that should be receiving medical attention.

Even though a female has been cleared medically to play, if a coach sees that she is nowhere near the level she needs to be – this must be addressed with more conditioning and training before allowing the athlete to play again. Physical therapists usually do not have the time to have an athlete perform functional sport training during rehab (as insurers are not paying for this). Physical therapists, athletic trainers, and specialists like me are available post-medically to bridge the gap between the end of health insurance coverage for rehab and preparing to play a sport.

In the past five to ten years, concussions (See Appendix C) from sports participation are being addressed and coaches need to follow the newest guidelines and new state laws that are being developed.

TOP TEN REASONS TO
FIRST FOCUS ON THE LOWER BODY
Top Ten Reasons for BNP Training

10. It is not a fad.

More than thirty years of research has determined that BNP training [other quality training programs may have different names] is
necessary for the many reasons listed on the www.learn2trainsafely.
com website.

9. Females are looser.

Female joints at adolescence are looser [more lax] than males at the
same age.

8. Females have challenges at puberty.

Prior to puberty, females and males are quite similar. This is why
researchers are now calling for lower body training from nine to
twelve years of age so that muscle memory is locked in before the
teenage years. We do not want to have young women facing an
osteoarthritis challenge (for more than 70% of females who injure
their ACL) within twelve years of the injury.

7. Historically, males have trained to play sports and females have not trained.

Males have trained to play their sports. By valuing training to play sports for all female athletes as the next step in their evolution, proper training will help the youngsters overcome the inherent challenges that occur at puberty.

6. Youth athletes do not get enough time off to let their minds and bodies recover.

Pros take four to eight consecutive weeks (or more time) off to rest physically and mentally before preparing for their seasons. Youngsters with open growth plates (i.e., growing bodies) need at least this amount time off from playing sports. A year round, periodized (best planning scheduler for sports) training program with proper rest periods will help every athlete avoid overtraining.

5. Youth coaches do not allow time off like pros do.

Youngsters with growing bodies need more time off than professional, mature athletes. Youth become one-sport athletes at an early age, and many do not cross-train their bodies resulting in repetitive motion injuries at too young an age, per health care professionals.

4. Student-athletes are invincible

Everyone thinks that female (and male) student-athletes will not suffer a major injury due to the joint (s) being overused without training to play the sport. All evidence-based research shows this is not the case. It is just the opposite with non-contact ACL injuries as the major injury challenge for all females.

3. Skills training.

Youth coaches, who are usually volunteers, do not understand the demands on the athlete's growing body that year round sports produces. Skills training is valued over training to play sports.

2. Lack of cross training.

Most female athletes play a single sport, and without proper training to play sports, the repetitive motions from a young age take a toll on their growing bodies.

1. More is known today than ever before about safe and age-appropriate training.

> Safe and age-appropriate training makes a significant difference in female athletic performance and minimizes the risk of injury when used as a preseason training program with a dynamic warm-up when practicing and playing competitively. The athlete makes her gains during their training and needs to maintain those gains during her season.

The BNP program has been tweaked several times. A salient feature comes from a University of Pittsburgh workshop (Lephart, Henry. 1997) that showed the flexed (bent) knee position for training was much better than the straight knee for performing balance, neuromuscular control, and proprioception [per Lephart and Fu in 2000 – enhancing the sensorimotor system] — the main elements of our BNP Training Program.

> "It was suggested that when the knee is flexed the hamstrings become better positioned to stabilize the tibia and

reduce anterior [forward] translation. The compensatory maneuver increases moments at the hip and knee, necessitating greater activity of the quadriceps to maintain stability."

"The effect of **coactivation on reducing anterior tibial displacement also suggests that knee flexor muscle activity may reduce the load on the ACL during knee extension** [five research studies cited here]." (Osternig L. Lephart and Henry 1997 workshop at U of Pittsburgh)

In the same workshop, a paper was presented that discussed proprioception and mechanoreceptors in the knee joint:

"Awareness of the body and its relationship with the surrounding environment is mediated through the phenomenon of sensation."

"Proprioception can be considered a specialized variation of the sense of touch and encompasses the sensation of joint movement and joint position in space. These modalities originate by stimulation of specialized nerve endings referred to as mechanoreceptors... All receptors are maximally stimulated immediately after a new stimulus is detected."

Mechanoreceptor function is described as "provid[ing] **position sense or conscious awareness of the joint in space, and they initiate protective reflexes that help to stabilize the joint and avoid injury**." (Barrack R, Barry Munn B. Lephart and Henry 1997 workshop at U of Pittsburgh)

Today, what I call BNP Training (other quality programs may have a different title) is widely accepted as the best way for female athletes to train their lower body. Even if you do not choose my BNP Training Program, please find a quality program that will help your daughter-athlete prepare her body for the demands of her sports.

IF THIS TRAINING IS FOR REAL, WHY DON'T WE KNOW ABOUT IT?

Evidence-based research will provide insights into the challenges when trying to implement training programs. Dr. Cynthia LaBella, Medical Director, Institute for Sports Medicine; Associate Professor of Pediatrics, Northwestern University Feinberg School of Medicine said (in a 2011 article about her research for teen female athletes) that getting coaches to change is difficult.

"Some coaches might not want to use the warm-up program because it takes time out of already limited practices", LaBella and her colleagues said. Along those lines, "coaches that were instructed to do warm-ups as usual, without learning the exercises, generally didn't do them at all or had athletes do warm-ups themselves" (when researchers develop a program they use a control group who perform the recommended exercises and a second group that uses the coach's normal program and the results are compared).

"Coaches oftentimes are hesitant to take practice time away from skill development," LaBella told Reuters Health. "They may only get the gym for an hour." But, she continued, "We really feel like it should be a routine part of sports training for teenage girls. It's worth the investment."

In the same article Tim Hewett, Ph.D. said the "warm-up exercises, when done correctly, can improve jumping height and power – not just prevent injuries. That's one way to sell them to coaches," he said.

"You can make a huge difference in the athleticism of these girls," Hewett said. "There are many ways we can show these kids that they're faster, quicker, and more balanced athletes.""

My warm-up program (1995 – 2011) has many of the same exercises that Dr. LaBella used in her research. Her new research is in addition to programs like the PEP Program (Mandelbaum, B, M.D., et al; first year in 2000) that have been helping female athletes for many years.

Look at what was said many years ago about the PEP Program:

"When discussing the nature of the PEP Program for ACL injury prevention, the training that is implemented into the curriculum is seeking to primarily address the feed forward mechanism — **to anticipate external forces or loads to stabilize the joint, thus protecting the inherent structures**. Several research studies have indicated proprioception may play a major role in injury reduction." (Kirkendall and Garrett. 2000)

The CEU courses for the safe training of adolescent female athletes at www.issaonline.com (have educated trainers since 2003) and other quality training programs specifically developed for teen (and older) female athletes are not enough to help as many as an estimated ten million young female athletes playing sports in the

United States. Recreation leaders need to help by insisting that the volunteer coaches take certification courses to prepare them for coaching today's female athletes. As previously mentioned, many years ago a recreation leader told me he was afraid that a several hour course would be too much for the coaches and that they would go elsewhere if the township had such a requirement to use their facilities.

Adults must realize that what Dr. Wojtys said many years ago is an important part of the messages that all health care professionals and researchers are trying to inform adults and their daughter-athletes about: "female athletes should not expect injury as a result of play-ing sports."

Now is the time for adults to learn, understand, and appreciate the differences that occur at puberty for their daughter-athlete. Then, take the next step and prepare their female athlete's body to play sports. The Darwinian approach – 'the strong will survive' with the one sport athlete from an early age has resulted in the current too high non-contact ACL injury rate.

LEARN2TRAINSAFELY.COM is developing a two year certifica-tion courses for volunteer coaches of female sports. It is my hope that over time, this added knowledge can help volunteer coaches minimize the risk of injury for our female athletes.

LEARN FROM AN OUTSTANDING FEMALE ATHLETE

The following is the perspective of a female student-athlete, Devon Keefe Wible, who graduated from Princeton University in 2001. She was an outstanding softball player — four-time All-Ivy honors at Princeton plus she was the All-Florida State catcher in both her junior and senior years in high school. I had the privilege of working with the Princeton University Tigers softball team during the 1999 college softball pre-season and season. Everyone interested in helping female athletes can benefit from Devon's insight.

The Life of a Student-Athlete

"The life of a student-athlete at any level is grueling. At times, we ask our bodies to perform the unimaginable. We play through pain in the relentless pursuit of victory. Throughout my fourteen-year career, I played softball, basketball, ran track, and threw the discus. I enjoyed every part of my athletic life including practice and training. It was never easy, but I loved the challenge and the competition.

I began playing sports after watching my brother play baseball. I was only eight years old, but I wanted to be out there with the boys playing in the dirt while my parents cheered for me. I joined him on the YMCA tee-ball team and soon found myself lost in all of the rules and confusion. I played second base and did not understand how to get someone out. I did not know that there were three outs per team per inning or even what an inning represented. Over time I learned the rules, changed sports, and began to play a new position. I no longer joined the boys on the diamond; I now played softball with the girls. I began playing slow-pitch softball when I was ten. Slow pitch was not as much fun as baseball, but I learned the rules and began to play catcher. I quickly grew bored of the arch pitching and the slow pace of the game. In an effort to find more excitement, my parents signed me up for fast-pitch softball. By this time, I was eleven years old, and tall and strong for my age.

Luckily, I was blessed with natural talent. I was a standout player and made the all-star team after my first season. For the first time in my life, I felt pressure to perform. The competition was better, and I was not one of the best players. I vowed that I was going to work even harder to improve my skills and that next year when I came back to the all-star tournament I would be the best. I worked with my father in the garage at least three times per week on my swing. I watched myself in the mirror and I began attending baseball camps and clinics with my brother. I was always the only girl at the camp, so I earned special attention from the instructors and other players. Because of their extra time, I began to show marked improvement.

All of my hard work paid off and when I was twelve; a coach approached me about playing on a traveling softball team. I was overjoyed at the prospect of traveling throughout Florida playing softball against better competition. The team paid for my expenses and we faced solid competition. I hit against and caught for better pitchers than I did in Little League. Plus, I enjoyed traveling and playing against different teams every weekend.

The schedule was grueling and softball became a year-long activity. There were two little league seasons — fall and spring. We practiced twice a week and also played two times. During the summer and winter, I practiced at least twice per week for my summer ball team and traveled nearly every weekend. In sixth through eighth grades, I also ran track for my middle school. I was a sprinter and practiced three times per week and participated in weekly meets. I was also heavily involved in academics. I loved going to school, and I almost always received the highest marks. I was in honors-level courses and in a special gifted program.

My work ethic remained with me into high school. I continued to work hard to become a better all around player. I worked out in the garage with my dad hitting wiffle golf balls with a sawed off broomstick. My brother and I would play our own version of stickball in our backyard where we set up a tee and soft-toss station. Again, my hard work and dedication to the game earned me respect and many honors. As a freshman, I was named first all-central Florida, all-league, and all-area as a catcher. My batting average was one of the highest in the state, and I led my region in almost every offensive category.

In my sophomore year of high school, I decided to also play basketball. Basketball did not come as easily to me as softball. I had really never played it before, and I found the basic skill of dribbling difficult. I did not know what a lay-up was on my first day of practice. Luckily, I was in great shape and could out run and outlast everyone on the court. I was the captain of the JV team and loved every second that I spent on the court. I improved every day at practice, and I loved game time.

Over the next two years, I improved on the basketball court and on the softball field. In my free time, I hit at the batting cages (at least fifteen rounds per week) and dribbled basketballs in my garage blindfolded. I also worked out with a personal trainer three times per week and did cardio an additional two to three hours per week. I enjoyed training and lifting. I felt like a better, stronger player when I was in the batter's box or on the court. It was a great feeling, one that kept me in top shape throughout my career.

Because of my superior play in high school, I was recruited by some of the best summer teams in Florida. I decided to play with the eighteen-and-under Clearwater Lady Bombers when I was fifteen years old. We traveled throughout the United States playing softball and gaining exposure to different college coaches. Over one hundred programs recruited me, including Florida State, University of South Florida, University of Massachusetts, and the University of Kansas. It was a hard decision, but I finally decided on Princeton University because of their high academic and athletic standards.

Playing sports at Princeton was not easy. The academic standards were greater than I expected, and I found myself in over my head during the first semester. I played softball, worked ten hours per week in the dining hall, wrote for the campus paper, and tried to keep up with a rigorous academic schedule. Softball and conditioning acted as a release for my high stress levels. I used lifting and conditioning to energize my day, and my time on the field was always a refreshing break from my hectic life.

College softball demanded more time, energy, and concentration than high school and summer ball. I also had to work extra hard in the classroom to keep my grades up. Over time, I grew accustomed to my new life and began to manage my time better. By no means was it an easy adjustment, but it was one of the most important lessons that I learned through my involvement with sports.

My four-year collegiate career had ups and downs. Unfortunately, I injured the balls of my feet my freshman year and the problem went undiagnosed for almost two years. I never had to play through so much pain and discomfort. The pain affected every part of my life. I could not run, it hurt to walk, and the doctors had me taking high doses of anti-inflammatories. The pain also affected my performance on the field. As a catcher, I was required to spend a lot of time on the balls of my feet, which was very painful. I could not move as well or run as fast. I struggled mentally to understand my limitations and to accept that I had them at all. With the help of a strength trainer and a sports psychologist, I learned to deal with my injury and still perform to my highest standards.

I continued to work hard in college to be one of the best players. I wanted to be the strongest, fastest, and hardest working person on the team. I always set high goals for myself and did not accept failure. I worked hard on the field, practiced in my extra time, pushed myself in the gym, and in the classroom. It was never easy, but in the long run it was always worth it!

As a female athlete, proper training played a key role in my success. In high school and college it was essential that I be in top condition to perform to my peak potential. As I matured, lifting weights and cross training became a major part of my life. During my sophomore year in college I began to train with Warren Potash. He introduced me to an entirely new way to train my body without causing injury, extreme fatigue, or over-training.

For the first time I realized that proper training is not only about working harder than everyone else, but it is also about working smarter than everyone else. In order to accomplish this, Warren utilized a variety of techniques such as cross-training and strenuous pool workouts that provided a full-body workout without the pounding that running caused to my joints. I also began to lift seriously and correctly for a female athlete. Lifting weights combined with cross training pushed my play to an entirely new level. Without proper training, I think that it would be virtually impossible to become a top athlete.

My fourteen-year athletic career has turned me into a strong, independent woman. I learned the value of leadership skills, the ability to multi-task, and how to manage my time effectively. Sports also helped me get into the best school in the nation, meet amazing people who will be my friends for life, and learn the importance of strength and cardiovascular training. I look forward to continuing my involvement in the athletic and academic world both as a coach and a teacher." (Devon N. Keefe, 2001 after graduating from Princeton University)

Devon at Princeton U

WHAT YOU CAN DO TO
HELP YOUR DAUGHTER-ATHLETE

LEARN, TRAIN, PERFORM

You cannot expect your young daughter to have the understanding to determine when, and if she needs to train to play sports. You have taken a first step by reading this book and becoming familiar with the challenges for all adolescent female athletes.

STATISTICAL EVIDENCE

I have found the following, reliable statistics from several different Internet sources and news articles:

- The type of ACL injuries; i.e., seventy percent are non-contact for female athletes.
- Each year, one out of 100 high school female athletes and one of 10 college female athletes experiences an ACL injury.
- The National Collegiate Athletic Association (NCAA) reports that in any given year, approximately 2,200 collegiate female athletes are expected to rupture their ACL.
- Based on these statistics, research shows that women have a three to nine times higher incidence of knee injury than their male counterparts.
- One ACL surgery and rehab costs are about 20,000 to $25,000 per patient. Combined, high schools and colleges are spending over $100 million [I have read total estimated

costs of more than $600 million annually in the United States (Hirst S, January 2007) per year on ACL reconstruction surgeries for female athletes.

MYTH – EVERY TRAINER CAN TRAIN A TEEN FEMALE ATHLETE

In theory, every trainer should have the knowledge to prepare a safe and age-appropriate training program for female athletes. However, many trainers do not fully appreciate the unique challenges that necessitate a different progression of exercises for adolescent female athletes.

Therefore, key considerations for selecting a one-on-one or group training program for your daughter-athlete are:

- What is the track record of the program?
- Are there evaluations from prior participants that support its methods?
- Does the program use a periodization* approach and is it well documented for review prior to training?
- What is the basis for a custom training program for an athlete?
- Is there a file for each athlete with her medical history, baseline assessment in key areas, and releases for program participation from the medical provider?
- Does the trainer have the proper credentials, experience, and training to work with an adolescent female athlete?
- Does the trainer come out to your daughter's games and watch her play several times during the season to make certain that her conditioning program translates onto her field of play?
- With high school, travel ball, homework, and other activities, does the trainer understand how to work with an ath-

lete so that she first takes care of business in the classroom and other important commitments?

♦ Periodization — a form of planning to produce a safe training program. The key to this organized planning schedule is that after an athlete progresses to a new level, she is stepped down to recover while training with the second and subsequent peak(s) are at a higher level then the previous one.

When evaluating a program for safely training your daughter, use all of the information contained in the www.learn2trainsafely.com position paper and then make age-appropriate decisions to maximize your female athlete's potential while minimizing her risk for injury and helping her to become the best student-athlete she can become..

SPORTS CHALLENGES FOR TEEN FEMALE ATHLETES

1. Knee and lower body injuries — most prevalent is the non-contact ACL injury.
2. Repetitive-motion injuries.
3. Developing functional joint stability is exactly what it implies. Leading researchers said: "the fact that simultaneous contraction of the agonisitic and antagonistic [opposing muscles where one is primary and the other supports] enhances the load imposed on and the stability of the joint stresses the importance of muscle coordination for functional joint stability" (Lephart, Fu 2000). This applies to all joints, not just the knee.

4. The growth plate (physis) is the area of developing tissue near the end of the long bones in children. Each long bone has at least one growth plate at each end. When growth is completed during adolescence, the growth plates are replaced by solid bone. When the growth plate is injured, osteoarthritis (OA) within 12 years can occur for seventy percent of the females who suffer an ACL injury, per valued research previously cited.

5. Female triad.

6. Not eating enough calories for their daily energy demands.

Injuries occur in children and adolescents. The growth plate is the weakest area of the growing skeleton, so a serious injury to a joint is more likely to damage a growth plate than the ligaments around it; except for the knee joint. Other injuries are:

a. Stress fractures — seen more often in runners and gymnasts.

b. Hip and knee injuries.

c. Ankle injuries.

d. Shoulder; rotator cuff for overhand sports.

"'Orthopedic surgeons insist that the problem is the "Q" angle at women's knees,' says Timothy Hewett, PhD, |in 2009| a professor of pediatrics and orthopedic surgery at the University of Cincinnati |now Tim Hewett, Ph.D., FACSM; Professor and Director of Research - Sports Health and Performance Institute at Ohio State University| and the Cincinnati Children's Hospital and is the lead investigator of the girl's case study. 'They think the problem begins because women's hips are wider' than men's. Other researchers have looked at the role of female hormones on tendon looseness in the knee." (NY Times, 2009)

Please realize that injuries are part of playing sports. The purpose of this book is to educate everyone how we can minimize the adolescent female's risk for injury; especially non-contact ACL injuries that are called the 'silent epidemic' by having all teen female athletes value training to play sports.

Notice that I never use the word *prevent*. I believe that we can only minimize the risk for injury with safe and age-appropriate training since injuries are an inherent risk of sports participation.

At www.learn2trainsafely.com you will find valuable information about the teen female athlete's sports challenges

Athletes cannot have fun when they are injured

PERSPECTIVES FROM A PHYSICAL THERAPIST

Bob Filer, Sports Medicine PT, is responsible for the training guidelines I have used since 1995. He was an athlete and he states his concerns about youth injuries:

"There is nothing more demoralizing to an athlete, female or male, than an injury. Usually, the more severe an injury is, the more demoralized the athlete becomes. An injury takes way the athlete's core strengths — the ability, talent, and skill to play their sport. An injury also takes away the mental and emotional aspects of sport's participation.

An athlete feels a void in her life when she cannot contribute to a game or help their teammates on the field. An injured athlete cannot feel the energy and drama of the game. An injury can take away the desire to compete.

After ACL surgery, the rehabilitation is demanding both mentally and physically. An athlete will wear a long leg brace for a few weeks. She must re-learn how to walk first before running begins. This athlete will not be able to start light jogging for about three months after the surgery. This is very hard for an athlete to handle, especially for those who were consistently "on the run." During, rehab, there are a series of progressions I put the athlete through to enable her to achieve the necessary functional goals for returning to their sport. The athlete will return to competition nine to twelve months after the ACL surgery.

That first year back is awkward both mentally and physically for an athlete. She will be thinking, "Is my knee going to give out?" "Can I pivot and change directions?" "Did I lose a step?" Not until the second year of playing after ACL surgery will the athlete become comfortable and stop thinking about her knee.

I feel a responsibility to alert the female athlete population that we have developed guidelines to help them minimize their risk for injury by training to play their sport. There is an old saying, "an ounce of prevention is worth a pound of cure." While no exercise program can guarantee the total prevention of injuries, as a healthcare professional and former athlete I know there is no downside to age-appropriate training. But there is always a risk of injury when a person plays sports.

As a physical therapist, it is very rewarding and fulfilling to help an athlete return to her field of play. In a perfect world, I would like each athlete to stay healthy and not be injured so she would not have to go through the arduous rehabilitation process.

Not too long ago, I was playing basketball and baseball competitively through high school and college. I hated to lose game time to an injury. I was afraid to tell the coaches I was hurt. Thankfully, there are many more effective training strategies available to an athlete than there were twenty or twenty-five years ago, lessening the chance for injury and helping to increase their personal level of play.

Adolescent female athletes, especially, should take advantage of the information that is now available to help them minimize their risk for injury. Due to the injuries I sustained during my career and the toll they took, I became a physical therapist so that I could help others learn how to take care of their bodies. Personally, I feel that helping athletes minimize their risk for injury is as rewarding as providing the rehabilitation itself.

If an athlete uses these |BNP Training Program| guidelines, it is because she wants to help herself. On the other hand, if she comes to me after the injury has occurred, it is because she now has to. Understanding and using the information in this book will help female athletes continue to experience the positive aspects of playing and competing in sports."

– Bob Filer, MS, PT, CSCS written in 2003

Once again, one of my colleagues words are as true today as when he originally wrote his thoughts about female athletes and sports injuries eight years ago.

I am presenting summaries of the interviews I conducted with two injured high school athletes so everyone can understand how a young woman thinks when she is injured, cannot play her sport and be with her teammates as an active team member.

A FEMALE STUDENT-ATHLETE SHARES HER PERSPECTIVE ABOUT SPORTS AND BECOMING INJURED REQUIRING SURGERY

ACL Injury – August, 2009

Diagnosis: Grade III ACL injury (complete tear) with meniscus tear requiring surgery

March 16, 2010: It is six and one-half months post-op and this athlete is just beginning to dribble a soccer ball, run in a straight line, and practice crosses. She says she is a 7/10 [70%] compared to being where she was prior to surgery. Since she is only 196 days post-op – attaining this 7/10 ability in a very timely manner, shows the determination and dedication she has to playing at the highest level again.

No one wants to focus on what ifs? Most athletes think they are invincible (an interesting thought from this young lady; she first saw soccer players tearing their ACL several years back, but it did not occur to her to train even though her club and high school teams changed their pre-practice routines). The mantra is: **injuries happen to others, I will be fine**. However, everyone can learn from a wise youngster who has been able to use her injury as a learning experience.

Previous to her injury in the summer of 2009, this teen earned a college scholarship to a top Division I soccer program (she is not losing her scholarship due to her injury). Without ever seeing her play – it is apparent that she is one of the most talented soccer players in the U.S. or she would not have received the athletic scholarship.

This young woman has amazing focus; i.e., she has the ability to block out negative thoughts and focus on figuring out: "what do I need to accomplish to be able to play at my pre-injury level again"? Was she ever down – of course; how could someone go from having fun playing their sport to not being able to play and facing surgery. The uncertainty at the start has given way to being able to see the light at the end of the tunnel.

In between – lots and lots of hard and smart training while maintaining her excellent grade point average in school. She really has her priorities dead-on straight.

The time between her injury and her surgery – approximately three weeks – are now a blur. It is amazing that humans can block out bad thoughts like this. Myself, having gone through three major surgeries in my life (last being January, 2009) – I know how a person can do this.

When she came home several days after her surgery, she spent four hours per day on a range of motion machine to begin to reduce the edema (and swelling) in her knee joint and to regain mobility; i.e., range of motion.

She could not watch her teammates practice/play during her rehab. She said: "my only thoughts throughout post-surgery rehab was that I had to get back to playing soccer at my highest level and eventually make up for my lack of playing time." Most athletes will rush back, but she was really thinking this process through every step of the way with her healthcare professionals guiding her progress. She listened to all of the adults in her life. Not just hearing what they say, but processing this information and helping to shape the strategy for her rehab. Trusting the professionals, she was determined to get back to playing the game she enjoys and sorely misses.

Matter of fact, she only rejoined her team when she was able to begin soccer skills training again. Regaining her ability to dribble, directional kicking including crosses, kicking for distance; all within the framework of a single plane of motion and with the knowledge that no one would run at her. Slowly, she is getting back to where she says she is a 7/10 at 6 ½ months post-op.

She can taste the air when she plays and she can feel the smell of the grass; the joy of getting back to playing again. When will she practice with her teammates for real and return to play – this remains to be seen. Amazingly, for a youngster (even though she is approximately 18 years old), her focus from her first post-surgery days has been to return when her body tells her she is ready. Slow and steady is her mantra. This is probably why she has been able to climb the ladder back to playing without a major/minor setback along the way. This is a tribute to not only this young woman, but to the therapist and doctor she is working with who have instilled the trust between them that is required to achieve her first goal; i.e., **return to play at her previous, elite level**.

She is using this as a learning experience; albeit, an experience she wishes she did not have so she could just be playing soccer. However, she has learned a lot; i.e., how to safely train so in the future she will know what to do, how to do it properly, how to strength train, etc. She sees this as a huge positive. She will know what to do and keep herself in the best shape possible. This, from an athlete who previously relied on her God given talent, and her passion to play soccer at the highest level possible.

April, 2010: I do not predict outcomes, but in this case – I will venture this opinion: I believe that with all that she has learned from this experience, this young woman will achieve all of her dreams and goals in the future.

Is it possible that her best playing days are in the rear view mirror? I seriously doubt this will happen. She has benefited from her sports participation and one day, when she has time to reflect about her soccer playing days – she will see that sports participation is really life skills training (as are all other pursuits that a person has a passion for).

She has learned that however mentally tough she was before the injury; she is much tougher mentally now than before. She knows she can handle adversity and turn a lemon type situation into lemonade. She has learned that it is how we choose to deal with what challenges we are given in our life is a matter of how well we can keep a positive outlook. She learned that she can face all of the negatives or hurdles facing her by using her strategic thinking skills to weave around all of the land mines (presented to her) and continue on the path to achieve her dreams and goals.

She is handling the process of injury, surgery and rehab, and now return to play. I believe she will agree that it is always best to:

Shoot for the Moon; you just might Reach the Stars.

A 2ND FEMALE STUDENT-ATHLETE SHARES HER PERSPECTIVE ABOUT HER KNEE INJURY

Diagnosis: Grade I (partial tear) PCL; no surgery

At March 22, 2010: Two and one-half months post-injury and this athlete is two weeks away from seeing her orthopedic doctor. The doctor will let her know the next steps.

At 15 ½ years young, the last thing you want to think about is: "what just happened to me"? "Why did this happen to me"? "Can I wear my dress and shoes to the big dance"? Yet, this is what happened to a young female soccer player; just having FUN playing her secondary sport – basketball – so she would be in great shape for the game she loves playing: soccer.

So, what does a person do? Let's find out how this young lady dealt with her circumstance(s).

She was injured playing for her high school basketball team and her knee blew up the next day. Two doctors offered different opinions about her injury. She and her family decided to stay with the doctor who took a more conservative approach for her PCL injury; i.e., return to play within six weeks or a return to play versus a 4 month option that she chose.

Going to physical therapy (PT), she was able to make sufficient early progress that she was able to pedal a bike (little or no intensity) and feel that her injured knee was as strong as her good knee within eight weeks of the day she was injured.

Her first thoughts were: "I was just injured playing basketball. Should I have been playing basketball when I really wanted to play varsity soccer" this Spring, 2010. Also, soccer players reminded her that she got hurt playing basketball. This just made it worse for her psychologically.

Teenage years should be a time where a person explores who she wants to be and begins a process to determine which values are most important. The last thing someone needs is for their peers to be questioning her judgment. Especially, when she had already been questioning them herself?

We can wake up one morning and slip in the bathtub or shower and crack a bone. Statistically, there is a chance that when we step into a vehicle to go for a drive – this is exposing us to potential danger.

It is unfortunate this injury occurred, but the reality is that if this had been a soccer injury – she still would not have been able to play soccer.

She has done a lot of soul searching. She has thought about what her goals need to be to be able to play again. She is even thinking about long term goals like playing in college and what needs to happen in the summer to make that a reality.

This a lot on the plate for a 15 ½ year old student-athlete; but, this is today's reality in the youth sports world. Today's youth take on adult concerns; whether their parents are encouraging this or not. They hear their teammates discussing these concerns and naturally, it will rub off on everyone. Especially, when a youth coach says to an athlete – come onto my team and collegiate coaches will see you in all of these tournaments we are playing in. In her own words:

"I am currently, and have been dealing with a coach… an hour away who wants me to play for his team. I guest play with them and have good friends on the team, but have not been ready to make a switch. It is really tough to have a coach you respect telling you that making that tough switch is the best option for your soccer career. I have decided that I am not switching this season, but I do think it is an issue a lot of girls deal with."

<u>May, 2010</u>: My hope is that she continues to make rapid progress (adolescents usually come back from injury quicker than adults) and with her health care professionals guidance, she is able to play sooner, rather than later.

I have presented the reaction of two teenage female soccer athletes who were injured and are taking the steps to once again play at the highest level each can attain.

Look at the excerpts from an article in 2009 (AAOS) that discusses what female athletes need to do to minimize their risk for injury when playing the sports they love to compete in so they can have FUN with the confidence they have prepared their body to withstand the demands of their physical activity.

AAOS ADVICE

The American Orthopedic Society for Sports Medicine has an initiative called *Sports Trauma and Overuse Prevention* (STOP) to lower the high rate of youth sports injuries. Please take a look at what specialists are calling for and appreciate what this organization is trying to accomplish:

> "Unfortunately, the trend towards early specialization in youth sports and the cultural pressures towards winning have resulted in increasing numbers of overuse injuries in children and adolescents.
>
> Children should not feel pressured to play when hurt. Signs of overtraining include:
>
> - stress fractures,
> - pain that does not improve with 2-3 days of rest, and
> - mental "burnout."
>
> To reduce the risk of overtraining:

- playing on multiple organized teams should be minimized and
- all athletes should have at least one season completely off [two plus months].

We must remember that the goals of sports are physical and emotional health. Fun and the joy of participation are more important than winning and being the best."

– www.STOPSportsInjuries.org

An orthopedic surgeon in Boston, MA has developed a way for adults and their daughter-athletes and coaches and trainers to know when to seek medical attention for a sports injury; the 3 S rule:

"If [injury] symptoms interrupt the 3 S's —
sleep, stride (limping, for example) or study,
[the athlete] needs to be checked out by a medical expert."
(O'Brien M)

You must understand that another leading orthopedic surgeon has been quoted saying that he cannot believe the internal damage he sees when he operates on a youngster. The damage is what he used to see when operating on adults for similar injuries (both females and males).

You may ask the question: why would orthopedic surgeons want to limit the number of surgeries performed on any segment of the population? One leading surgeon said: "it's the right thing to do." (Geier CD Jr,)

Nutrition for Daily Energy

Since 1995, I have taught teen female athletes about eating for daily energy and sports participation as part of the integrated training program. Female athletes have to be taught how to properly fuel their body for their busy days. They need energy for studying, playing their sport, a social life, their family life, and whatever else each female athlete decides is important during her teenage years. Usually, they underestimate the amount of calories they need every day.

A major challenge for today's teen female athlete is disordered eating. This is not the same as eating disorders, which have received much attention. Therefore, before a discussion of eating for daily energy can be presented, you need to familiarize yourself with the disordered eating challenge.

MYTH — DISORDERED EATING IS NOT A MAJOR ISSUE
Dr. Karen Reznik Dolins wrote *In the Dark*, that, in my opinion, has made the difficult subject of disordered eating understandable. Most people have heard of "eating disorders." Disordered eating is much more subtle, as Dr. Dolins points out. She writes: "disordered eating is recognized as a spectrum, with eating disorders heading [the list]."

What is disordered eating? It is not only the female triad or eating disorders, that is, anorexia nervosa, bulimia, binge-eating disorders, which most people have heard about. Dr. Dolins says, "Our athletes have gotten the message that they need to eat to power their bodies, but they still don't have a clear concept of how to eat to fuel themselves while maintaining an optimal body weight."

For more than sixteen years, whenever I have taught the sports nutrition part of the training, teen female athletes have never guessed the correct answer to the following question: How many calories do you need on days that you train hard for an hour or more?

The correct answer is (as a generalization since the amount of extra calories should be calculated for each person): 150 percent or more of your daily calorie need for activities of daily living (ADL) when counting exercise demands. A 120-pound female may need about 1,500 calories daily on non-exercise/training days, but on training days (or hard practice days of 60 minutes or longer) this would be 2,250 calories or more. There are usually the following responses from a group of young ladies: "No way! Are you kidding me? I will get fat."

This is why Dr. Dolins writes: "[Athletes] are confused about how strict a diet should be, and they don't understand the balance between eating healthy and 'fun' food. **Athletes need significantly more energy to support their high level of activity.... athletes who may easily be burning 500 to 1,000 calories or more daily during training often fail to accommodate for their extra energy needs with a corresponding increase in calories consumed, resulting in low energy availability**."

Athletes who suffer from disordered eating and their coaches and trainers need to listen to Dr. Dolins as she writes: "the **challenge is to help these athletes regain their trust in themselves and allow their bodies to tell them how much food they need to eat**. The goals for this athlete are to:

- Have the confidence to eat when they feel hungry and stop when they feel satisfied.
- Understand that eating is primarily done to provide nutrition, but is also pleasurable and it's okay to eat something simply because it tasted good.
- Be aware of the need for energy balance, but not consumed by the fear that you are exceeding it.
- Be able to eat without feeling that food choices define self-worth."

She concludes with: "Athletes deserve to take pride in their accomplishments. Body dissatisfaction should not be used as a motivator for change. **Rather, coaches and athletic trainers can play a key role in the development of healthy eating behaviors by motivating athletes to take care of their bodies, understand the nutritional demands of the sport, and acknowledge the need to provide the best fuel possible**."

I was fortunate to have several outstanding RD's help produce a sports nutrition course (Appendix A: Sport Nutrition Guidelines) that has helped female athletes since 1995. You can read Dr. Dolin's entire article and find other resources at: www.TRAINING-CONDITIONING.COM. (Dolins KR, November 2010)

At www.learn2trainsafely.com you can learn about proper eating for daily energy and your daughter-athlete can begin to appreciate that 1,250 – 1,500 grams of calcium (yogurt, milk, and cheese are good sources) is needed each day during the teenage years so strong bones are formed to serve them for the rest of their life. Females build bone strength during the teenage years to help them avoid osteoporosis as they age.

- Learning what and how often to eat and drink is important to keeping each youngster hydrated, even more so for the demands of hot weather. Did you know that even a two percent decrease in hydration leads to an exponential decrease in performance? An athlete cannot wait until she feels thirsty; she needs to learn how to properly hydrate her body. She needs to know what she should be eating before, during, and after practices and games. She should not wait until game day to try something. She should use training and practice time to learn what works for her.

- If a coach says that holding back on food or water is a sign of mental toughness; this is a signal that the coach needs to be educated, or needs to stop coaching before he/she hurts a young athlete.

There is a 30 minute to 2 hour window to eat after practicing and competing for an athlete to maximally replenish her muscles.

Understanding Fundamental Training Concepts

To introduce fundamental training concepts, I am going to first address a **myth**: **My daughter-athlete will not get hurt; injuries happen to others.** *False!*

Teens think they are invincible — someone else will be injured, not me. This type of thinking is prevalent among both adults and athletes.

You need to appreciate the benefits of training to minimize the challenges that female athletes face when practicing and playing games. Then, everyone needs to value safe and age-appropriate training so every female can become a better athlete and minimize her risk for injury by stabilizing and strengthening her joints and core; not just relying on skills training.

Power formula

Power = Strength X Speed [or Flexibility [Range of Motion]]

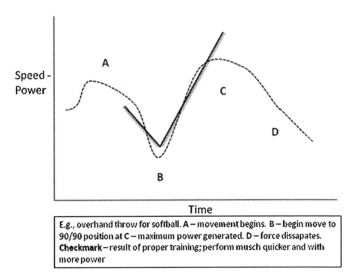

POWER CURVE – all muscular movement

E.g., overhand throw for softball. A – movement begins. B – begin move to 90/90 position at C – maximum power generated. D – force dissapates. **Checkmark** – result of proper training; perform musch quicker and with more power

This equation is important to understand for all adults who are working with athletes. Graphically, a sideways S-type curve describes all human muscular movement. A trainer needs to move this curve toward the checkmark in a safe and age-appropriate manner when training every female athlete to optimize their sport speed, quickness, agility, and strength. This is a major consideration when preparing safe exercises and drills for every female athlete.

To perform optimally, an athlete will want to enhance her fast-twitch muscle development for all sports. Therefore, the S-type curve will give way to a checkmark. Or, as the Nike swoosh logo and words describe, athletes need to "just do it."

The result of foundation training for the lower (and upper) body is for all joints to work optimally so that safe and age-appropriate power can be generated without over-stressing the athlete's body. For increased speed, teenage female athletes require increased hamstring strength. They need to learn how to increase their stride. Over the course of training, they should be able to have a sprint stride equal to 90 percent to 110 percent of their height. For example, if the youngster is 66" tall, her trained stride length will be approximately 59.4" to 72.6". It is important to realize this is just an average. Leg turnover rate increases as the ratio between the female's quads and hamstrings is closer to 66 2/3 percent and she performs stretching regularly. Most untrained female athletes begin at 38 percent to 42 percent.

The entire kinetic chain must be addressed during training; for the lower body the adolescent female athlete must train her trunk and lower body, as well as her core. This is necessary because non-contact knee injuries are so prevalent among teenage female athletes. Hip exercises are always needed as an integral part of this BNP training.

Closed kinetic chain vs. open kinetic chain exercises. Closed chain exercises are the easiest to perform and each female athlete must progress to being able to perform her exercises in an open chain.

Definitions:

Kinetic chain refers to concept that the body is interconnected. E.g., the ankle is affected by the foot. The knee is affected by the ankle... going up toward the top of head.

Closed-chain is a training method where a body part during exercise is always in contact with a stable surface. E.g., the knee is injured and in early training (or rehabilitation) the floor is the stable surface so the foot never loses touch with the floor to best support the knee through its range of motion.

Open-chain is the opposite of closed-chain activities: contact with a stable surface does not occur. E.g., full knee extension; sitting on a table edge and lifting the leg with control.

Training the tendons and ligaments first is the only way to fully develop the teen female athlete so she is better balanced. She will optimize her proprioceptive ability with neuromuscular control of her joint.

Growth plate issues are one of the most important considerations when determining how to advance every youngster during strength training. Premature strength development can prevent complete bone growth (open growth plates) and can have adverse long-term implications, i.e., a possible future arthritis site.

Therefore, I use a question in the medical history to help answer this question for the female athlete. When did menstruation begin? Did breast development come before or after puberty?

Answering these questions can help in determining when growth plates have matured and closed without expensive medical testing. If a teen female athlete's breast development started prior to puberty (Mom usually remembers if the athlete does not or have them look at family pictures) – her growth plates will usually close by fourteen to fifteen years of age [usually the bigger breasted female]. The slender body type, usually with smaller breasts, will have growth plates that remain open until 18 years of age (Schinfeld, J, M.D. 1995).

A "path" (progressions) is followed for each athlete to minimize her risk for injury during training. Custom training programs for each athlete are based on her individual assessment as determined by testing. The progressions then used will ultimately determine the effectiveness of the program. Proper technique for performing exercises and the use of stretching and increasing ROM (range of motion) for the joints play critical roles in helping the female athlete minimize her risk for injury.

My recommended requirements for building a foundation training program for an athlete are:

1. Medical history, medical clearance, and parent consent before beginning the exercise program.
2. Female athlete assessment by trainer.
3. Discuss POWER formula with female athlete so she understands how speed, agility, quickness, and stamina are enhanced by safe training.
    a. Age-appropriate training discussion.
4. BNP Training
5. Core strength developed.
6. Flexibility is developed.
    a. Ligaments and tendons trained before, or at same time as strength training.
7. Core strength including low back stabilization and strengthening; i.e., a spine-safe approach that translates

onto the field of play and in activities of daily living |ADL| (or some know this as a neutral spine).

8. Strength is developed over time; SLOW RATE/LOW WEIGHT works best for the majority of young female athletes with two sets of 12 – 15 reps.

9. Optimal balance, neuromuscular control, and proprioception are developed <u>before every new season</u>.

As stated, first-time athletes training should "go low, go slow." Please realize that "Rome was not built in one day." **Less can be more** until each athlete masters all the movements. In fact, less can be more will always be an important issue when training the vast majority of adolescent female athletes.

How do you know when a teen female athlete can advance? When the athlete can perform the last two reps of the last set as easily as the first two reps of the first set – advance to the next weight and do not exceed a ten percent increase in weight.

SAFE AND AGE-APPROPRIATE TRAINING PROGRAM

A functional and sport-specific training program will enable a female athlete to safely accomplish her goals if she follows certain guidelines. Becoming the best student-athlete is a key component for playing sports as an adolescent.

Most females want to develop lean muscle at the end of their program. To accomplish this, the following guidelines are used:

- training with low weight (60% of the 1 RM max unless there is a medical challenge). E.g., an athlete pushed 100 lbs as her 1 RM max (or use 2 or 3 max test) for the leg press so she will begin with 1 set of 15 reps at 60 lbs.

- slow rate (12 - 15 reps per set), and
- cardio – submaximal (60% to 85% PE) interval training
  NOTE: Intensity during training does not exceed 8 ½
  PE (on a 0 to 10 scale)

This will lead to the following benefits:

- lean muscle mass will burn more calories,
- increased metabolism and bone density,
- better body composition,
- decreased resting blood pressure,
- improve the body's ability to function, and
- increased muscle size.

Plyometrics with no depth jumping (until late intermediate to advanced stage of training is attained) is recommended and each female must be taught proper running and jumping technique to reduce the risk for ACL injuries:

- Running – 5° to 10° of forward lean (as measured from the ankle to the shoulders); i.e., very slight lean with the ball-heel technique,
- Jumping – recruiting their hamstrings to jump and landing SOFTLY on the balls of their feet with their knees flexed (bent), and
- Cutting – knees never go beyond toes or track inside or outside of the toes; the center of the knee always tracks between the first and 2nd toes.

Sports' participation during youth and adolescence teaches them life's lessons in a sports setting. Athletes must learn how to manage their time effectively so sports can be integrated into their busy schedules. They require the discipline to follow all at home exercises required and each female must take responsibility for her training her body to play sports.

ADOLESCENT FEMALE ATHLETE TRAINING INCLUDES:

1. Warm-up, stretching, strength, cardio, with a cool-down.
   a. 5 minute warm-up prior to stretching.
   b. 12–15 second stretches.
   c. Sub-maximal |60% to 85% perceived exertion (PE) interval training for cardio.
   d. Cool-down with light stretching.
   e. Hydrate during training; stay ahead of becoming thirsty.

2. Athlete never holds her breath when training
   a. Exert = Exhale; Resting phase = Inhale.
   b. Know when to exert. E.g., bicep hammer curl. Exhale when bringing weight or resistance tubing up and inhale and when extending weight forward with control.

3. When the first two reps of the first set are as easy, and each rep is performed perfectly as the last two reps of the second set; advance to next level with no more than a 10% increase in weight.
   a. Recommended: two sets of 12–15 reps each
   b. If two reps are too difficult, STOP.
      b-1. E.g., if you perform 6 curls and the next two are difficult, STOP. After a few minutes, try again. If it is too difficult, try to increase forty-eight hours later; set the goal as reaching the seventh rep or beyond

4. Advanced training – e.g., when jumping always land with soft knees; i.e., bend in knees, never stiff
5. Forty-eight hours of rest in between strength training for the same body parts. When plyometrics are added as advanced exercise, take 72 hours rest between workouts.
6. Apply periodization training principles. Simply stated, this means do not have back-to-back hard workouts. Cycle through easy, medium, and hard workouts.
7. RESULT: Thinking during training. Acting and reacting during games while thinking ahead before athlete is involved in play. The trained athlete's performance increases; i.e., translates into better athleticism.

However, this does not mean that everyone will be the best athlete. It means that an athlete will be better than before she began training.

Dr. Harber says: "training programs are not a one size fits all" proposition. Every female athlete will have differences that must be addressed – even in group training. Please realize that a one time training program will provide very good results for one season. Therefore, the following mantra must be used before every season:

MAKE YOUR GAINS IN THE PRESEASON and MAINTAIN YOUR GAINS DURING THE SEASON.

All adults and their daughter-athlete will ask: when is my season? Now, you understand why year-round play has caused so many injuries. There use to be a high school season and you made sure you were prepared for that season. Now, there are many volunteer coaches who encourage their best players to "blow off" the high school season since they promise their program as the best exposure for their athletes to be seen by college coaches.

In my day – the college coaches found you. Now, parents will spend lots of money to get in front of college coaches. Usually, it does not work. Whether it is youth coaches at all levels, alumni or friends – college coaches begin zeroing in early and watch a player she/he is interested in over time.

AVOID BURNOUT FROM OVERTRAINING

Too much training, practice, and play without proper rest can lead to overtraining; i.e., physical and/or mental burnout can occur. When you read about staying away from year-round sports, a leading reason is to avoid overtraining symptoms. Only a qualified physician can diagnose overtraining and/or burnout.

This is what a researcher states about preventing overtraining:

> "Tapering the training regimen with rest, proper nutrition, and sleep help the body heal.... Periodization of training with enough recovery should prevent overtraining if other stressors and their influence on recovery are also taken into consideration. Periodization means that correct loads of training stimuli are administered followed by adequate recovery periods. Periodization also diminishes the monotony of training when done over the long and short term."

> "The most sensitive physical parameters for following up of the training state and overloading seem to be changes in physical efficiency, mechanics, and coordination in addition to heart rate changes during maximal and submaximal exercise."

"Unless tapering and adequate recovery time is built into a training |practice and play also| schedule, overreaching can lead to overtraining |and burnout – mental and physical|. (Uusitalo ALT, May 2001)

PROPER NUTRITION

You must keep emphasizing to an adolescent female athlete that she needs more calories — about 150% more on average — on the days she trains hard (60 to 90 minutes or more in one day). Young women cannot believe they can eat the amounts of food (protein, carbs |carbohydrates|, fat, vitamins, minerals, and fluids) they really need to provide proper energy on a daily basis. They are afraid of gaining weight |Dolins K. *In the Dark.*|.

Determining the daily nutritional requirements for female athletes can be very complex for most teen female athletes. Young women need to learn how to eat for properly for daily energy.

If an adolescent female athlete is being trained for long distance running, swimming, etc., it can be more difficult to prepare a solid eating plan. If this way of eating is too big a challenge to implement, please realize that sport nutritionists are available to make certain a teen (and older) female athlete is getting enough energy on a daily basis. A depleted carbohydrate reserve plays a role in overtraining.

"A gradually depleting carbohydrate reserve with repeated strenuous training most likely contributes to the overtraining syndrome. It requires at least 1 to 2 days of rest or lighter exercise |usually longer| combined with a high carbohydrate intake to reestablish pre-exercise muscle glycogen levels after exhaustive training or competition. Unduly heavy exercise performed regularly requires an upward

adjustment of daily carbohydrate intake to optimize gly-
cogen resynthesis and high-quality training." (Gatorade
Sports Science Institute,1991)

Yes, 1991 research is still valid.

PERIODIZATION PLANNING FOR SPORTS

This is a subject that has to be studied thoroughly. It is not in the
scope of this information to fully explain this important topic that
trainers and coaches need to use. Athletes cannot be expected to
perform at their highest level for too long; i.e., usually a couple of
weeks is the longest an athlete can compete at a peak performance
level without suffering physical and/or mental burnout symptoms.
A trainer does not decide when to peak an athlete. It is a combined
effort where the coach, trainer, athlete, and parents all look at her
sports' schedule and then determine when the peaks need to occur
(parents will know family vacation and other important dates).

Please be aware this planning exists and make certain that every
trainer uses some form of this planning to ensure every female athlete's safety during training. This planning model is built on micro,
meso, and macro cycles; i.e., daily, weekly, monthly planning within
a predefined period of time with easy, medium, and hard training
sessions [e.g., 13 weeks, training 3 times per week].

The key to this organized planning schedule is that after an athlete
progresses to each new level, she is brought down a step and the
second and subsequent peaks are at a higher level than the previous
peak. In a 13 week training schedule there will be three peaks during the training. The first cycle will establish a strong foundation
for subsequent peaks. The last peak will optimally train the athlete
with safe and age-appropriate advanced exercises to fully train the

fast-twitch muscles and top off the cardiovascular training for the athlete's sport.

WHAT IS INTEGRATED SPORTS TRAINING?

An adolescent needs much more than just sport-specific skills, drills, and exercises. Her strength, flexibility, and cardiovascular training program must be integrated and coordinated with those drills and skill development, as well as proper rest. Using a core strength program at the beginning with sport-specific training will help each athlete be the best she can become.

This training must translate into becoming a better athlete on her field of play as compared to how she played prior to training. I am a firm believer that a trainer must go to several games to make sure the athlete benefitted from her training program. I guarantee my results. If the athlete needs more help, I provide it on my dime.

The International Sports Sciences Association [www.issaonline.com] notes that "integrated training is a delicate balancing act which involves the administration of several components — skill training, strength development, flexibility work, speed, agility, and quickness training. Strategy, motivation, nutrition, and many other [components]."

Simply stated a female athlete must develop strength and muscular endurance, ROM [range of motion], and cardiovascular (I recommend interval training) endurance leading to gains in power, speed, agility, and sport-specific skills.

Can every adolescent benefit from integrated training. Absolutely! My pre-season, sport-specific training program instructs each athlete in:

- Sports nutrition,
- Sports vision,
- Strategic thinking skills,
- Time management, and
- Mental toughness training — focusing between the lines.

Note: www.learn2trainsafely.com has quality information about each bullet point.

Conclusion

Taking the time to appreciate and understand the information presented in this book, you can see that health care professionals and researchers have known for many years what adolescent female athletes need to do to prepare their body for the demands of sports participation. Now is the time to implement what is known to help adolescent female athletes and discard the old time thinking and outdated approach for youth sports development for all female athletes.

Females cannot be trained as if they were males – their challenges must be appreciated and understood by all trainers who work with this teen population. Establishing a strong foundation with neuromuscular training is the best approach. In addition, Dr. Dot Richardson (U.S. Softball and Olympic gold medalist) and her colleagues, the American Academy of Orthopedic Surgeons and other researchers have been stating in the past years what I have been encouraging athletes to do for the past sixteen years: female student-athletes need to train to play their sport to minimize their risk for injury and to have fun trying to be the best each can become on and off their field of play.

One important training goal is that training for athletic competition should be a valuable part of preparing to play sports and all efforts must translate onto the field of play and in the classroom; i.e., the student-athlete must be emphasized first. Sports participation prepares a youngster for the rest of her life, and I want to be part of helping to improve the whole person for now and for their future endeavors; not just their game performances.

> "According to a study conducted by Timothy E. Hewett, Ph.D., comprehensive neuromuscular training is effective in improving measures of both performance and lower extremity biomechanics in adolescent female athletes. Dr. Kimberly Templeton also underscores the importance of girls understanding bone health.

> Dr. Hewitt offers this recommendation: "Here's the answer right now, if you are afraid that your daughter or your athlete might get into trouble, train her. Number one, it's going to decrease her likelihood of injury... Number two, it's going to make her a better athlete." (Templeton KJ, *March 2007*)

Every student-athlete is a winner. Winning is not reserved for the few who earn a championship trophy. Everyone is a winner when their preparation for playing sports leads to increased confidence in a young woman's ability to critically think through a challenge or the self-confidence that she can make it no matter what obstacles are thrown in her way. We know how to help every female athlete prepare her body for now and into the future with safe and age-appropriate training to play sports. Learning how to optimize her daily energy needs with proper nutrition and proper rest will serve her well now, and for the rest of her life.

Looking at the big picture, and not just focusing on wins and losses are what adults must do to ensure that their daughters' sports playing days help her accomplish all of her hopes and dreams; maybe even exceed them. This ensures that every female athlete will have a quality sporting experience. They need to enjoy and have fun during their sports participation days.

Therefore, to help all female athletes minimize their risk for injury and have fun playing their sport; the next hurdle is for all adults and their daughter-athlete is to

VALUE TRAINING TO PLAY SPORTS.

Afterword: Blue Shoes

Throughout history women have had to struggle for equality in all elements of society, but perhaps nowhere have they had a more difficult challenge than in sports. On June 23, 1972, Congress enacted Title IX of the Educational Amendments to the Civil Rights Act of 1964 which states that "No person in the United States shall, on the basis of sex, be excluded from participation in, be denied the benefits of, or be subjected to discrimination under any education program or activity receiving federal financial assistance." Although this legislation made no mention of sports, it has had a profound effect on opportunities available for girls and women in sports.

As far back as I can remember - I've always loved to be physically active. I grew up in a small Midwestern town where it was safe to play and play we did. Hide and seek on summer nights, racing on our bikes as far as we could go, swimming as fast as we could were things we loved to do. I also loved to run. In elementary school I could run faster than anybody else. I did dream about the Olympics. But growing up before Title IX was passed presented obstacles. My brother, who was 17 months older, had every opportunity to participate in any sport he chose.

In junior high we had an annual track and field day where we competed against other homerooms. They even kept records. It was not unusual for me to come home with all blue ribbons. I was so proud of those accomplishments. I haven't checked recently, but maybe some of those records still stand. The high school offered an

extensive Girls' Athletic Association (GAA) program and I participated in every activity accumulating more points than anyone else.
Some of us were chosen to represent our high school in a particular
sport at the local college. I was chosen to participate in the basketball contest. We were rated on skills and knowledge. I received a
1 rating. During the summer after my junior year in high school, it
was decided to start a competitive softball team. There were tryouts.
Over a hundred girls showed up to try out for one team that would
travel and compete with nearby towns. I made the team and played
first base and was the lead-off hitter. It was a great experience
competing against other teams!

I went on to college and received my Bachelor of Science in Education and the Master of Arts degree in Physical Education and Health.
During this time, I continued playing on intramural teams and running on my own. After graduating with my Master's degree I was
hired at the university to teach and be an assistant coach in volleyball and softball. The following year I accepted a teaching fellow-
ship at the University of Utah and continued my education as well
as my interest in sports for women.

The Association for Intercollegiate Athletics for Women (AIAW)
met at Park City, Utah, to discuss strategy for Title IX. I attended
those meeting and there was such an air of excitement that finally,
women were going to have the opportunities that men have enjoyed
as a birthright. I had the privilege of being named to a panel for
women in sport. It was also during this time that I ran in the gym.
People thought I was crazy. It was before "running shoes" for
women, so I used a men's pair of Adidas shoes. They were bright
blue; with reflecting yellow stripes.....I still have those shoes!

Title IX has given millions of women the opportunity to participate in sports. Research has shown the many benefits of participation. Female athletes are more likely to develop positive school
and lifestyle habits. Participation not only enhances academic
outcomes, but athletes miss less class time, are less likely to
smoke, drink or use illegal drugs, and are less likely to experience
an unintended pregnancy and eating disorders. They are also more
likely to have a positive body image than girls who don't participate in sports. Increasing physical activity can also help com-
bat childhood obesity. Other benefits include goal setting, time
management skills, learning to work as a team, and the ability to
overcome adversity. Many of our female leaders and CEOs have
a background in sports. Since the passage of Title IX, opportunities for females to participate in sports has led to a 400 percent
increase in the rate of female participation in college sports and a
more than 800 percent increase in participation at the high school
level (www.aauw.org).

Title IX has forever changed the landscape. It has given females
opportunities never before imagined. Would it have made a difference in my life? Possibly. I would have loved to have had the opportunity to participate competitively. But I remain active and have pursued my chosen profession – teaching and coaching.

The one thing I am most grateful for is that my daughter had the
opportunity to participate in sports. She played interscholastic and
intercollegiate sports and also got to coach and play overseas. She
had a wonderful career and continues to be active. AND her daughter will also reap the benefits of Title IX. Her son will also get to
participate in whatever sport he wants to play. My sons also got to
compete in sports and their sons will also get to participate. Isn't that

the way it should be? We all get to pursue our own dreams, whether female or male!

Thanks to Title IX! It has given women all the options they need to be the very best they can be!"

      – Janie Rider, Ph.D., Assistant Professor of Exercise Science
      California Lutheran University, Thousand Oaks, CA

Appendix A: Sport Nutrition Guidelines

It is beyond the scope of this book to include an entire nutrition section. The information below can help guide you, and you can learn more about energy for daily nutrition at www.learn2trainsafely.com.

NUTRITION FOR BEFORE, DURING, AND AFTER WORKOUTS

PRE-EXERCISE

    1. Eat adequate CARB (carbohydrate; CHO) snacks and meals and hydrate to fuel muscles

       1a. Snack = 60 to 90 minutes before exercise or playing

       1b. Meal = 2 to 3 hours before you play

HINTS:

- Limit HIGH FAT (1/3 of daily requirements) AND FIBER (more than 10 grams) ITEMS
- Be VERY CAUTIOUS of high sugar foods and juices

    2. DRINK plenty of Fluids!!

- Drink EXTRA water the day before to over hydrate (4 to 8 glasses)
- 2 to 3 hours before playing – DRINK 8 to 16 ounces BEFORE EVENT

A 2% Decrease in Hydration Status =

5%+ DECREASE IN PERFORMANCE

During the Event

1. DRINK every 15 minutes – DO NOT wait until you are thirsty – it will be too late!!

2. If exercising for 60 to 90 minutes or more – EAT some form of carbohydrate:

   • To provide energy
   • To help maintain blood sugar

   2a. BOTH OF THE ABOVE BULLETS CAN BE ACCOMPLISHED BY USING A SPORTS DRINK – if too high in carbs, then dilute with water and ADD a complex CHO to extend energy curve

Tournaments and Day Long Events

GOALS
   • Proper Hydration
   • Normal Blood Sugar
   • Fueled Muscles

Therefore, to achieve these goals, pack or order:
   • Grains
   • Fruits
   • Sports Drink or Bars

The NIGHT BEFORE the first game and for evening meal, EAT:

- Bread – 1 to 2 pieces (watch butter)
- Pasta with sauce (not too spicy or fatty) – 1 to 2 servings
- Protein – Couple of Meatballs, low-fat (3 oz.)
- Dessert - Fruit

BE CAREFUL WITH CARBS – TOO MUCH CAN
LEAVE YOU FILLING TOO FULL

Nutrition for Recovery (between games and after games for the day)

1. REPLACE CARBS (grains, fruit, milk – if can toler-
   ate milk) used during the event within 2 hours
   1a. It takes 20 hours to FULLY replenish muscles
   1b. Require .5 grams of Carbs per pound of body
   weight; e.g., a 130 lb. Female athlete = 65 grams of
   Carbs
2. REPLACE WATER – 2 cups for each pound lost during the day
3. REST!

HOT DAYS
- DILUTE Gatorade (or sports drinks) with ½ water – sports
  drinks have carbs – too much during the day will leave
  you bloated and slow; that is the reason for diluting these
  drinks.
- NO MORE than 300–400 calories from sports drinks/
  day (same reason as above); some sports drinks have 200
  CHO per bottle – READ information to make sure of CHO
  content.

- Hot, humid day – Have athletes REST in hotel. MUST lie down – not play games or go in pool.
- ½ Protein by Lunch; ½ Protein by Dinner; i.e., 3 oz. at each meal.
- Get to field 1 hour before playing to stretch and get reactivated to hot, humid weather.

SPORTS NUTRITION TIPS

Daily Food Requirements♦:

•	Carbohydrates	9 per day
•	Veggies	4–5 per day
•	Fruits	3 per day
•	Dairy	3 per day
•	Meat, Poultry, Fish	6 ounces per day
•	Fats	Sparingly

*Note: Protein, Fat, Carbs, Water, Vitamins, and Minerals are required on a daily basis.

♦This is for an average adolescent female and does not account for those days when practicing or playing for 60 – 90 minutes or longer

Appendix B: Challenges for Female Athletes at Puberty

This valued research information is so important to appreciate the differences at puberty between female and male athletes so I am repeating it here once more:

EVIDENCE-BASED RESEARCH

There is an unacceptably high injury rate for the female athlete, primarily due to non-contact anterior cruciate ligament injuries. These ACL injuries happen at a rate as much as three to nine times higher than male athletes (Gillette Children's Specialty Healthcare, December 3, 2010; research cited). Researchers have determined there are many reasons why female athletes are more prone to ACL injuries, including biomechanical, physiological, hormonal, and cognitive issues. Researchers say the reasons are complex and connected to the following:

- Absence of neuromuscular spurt at puberty♦ (as compared to males).
- Female triad — osteoporosis, eating disorders, and amenorrhea (loss of period).
- Wider hip to knee ratio ("Q angle") and pelvis is anterior (to the front) as compared to a male pelvis being towards the posterior (to the back).
- Jumping using quads and landing hard.
- Running upright.

- Possible hormonal changes.
- Muscular imbalances and weaknesses.
- Quadriceps dominance.
- Lax (loose) joints; i.e., properties of ligaments and tendons.
- Playing sports without training.
- Growth plate and joint development.
- Lack of coordination and fatigue.
- CNS [central nervous system] – Cognitive - Female Injury

✦ Many researchers believe the absence of the neuromuscular spurt for females at puberty is one of the more significant issues.

Appendix C: Concussions — Return to Play

At www.learn2trainsafely.com there is up-to-date information on concussions. If she suffers a concussion, it is important to understand this subject so you know your daughter is receiving the best care from a qualified physician.

In the May/June issue of *Training & Conditioning* magazine, Phil Hossler, MS, ATC (a NATA Hall of Fame inductee in 1999) presents a Concussion Assessment and Management Portfolio (CAMP), which he developed as a result of the three major changes on concussion safety and return-to-play criteria. (Also available at www. cdc.gov/concussion.)

He says that from the 2008 Zurich Concussion Conference, return to play programs should include the following stages:
1. No Activity
2. Light Aerobic Exercise
3. Sport-Specific Exercise
4. Non-Contact Training Drills
5. Full-Contact Practice
6. Return to Play

"In addition to neurocognitive testing, the Balance Error Scoring System (BESS) provides a … 10-minute series of tests." He further states that CAMP provides the documentation the athlete's physician needs to clear the athlete.

WORKING WITH PARENTS

Phil Hossler makes sure he uses three talking points when speaking with parents:

1. Complete Rest is Needed
2. Second-Impact Syndrome, Recurrent Concussions
3. Involve teachers as part of the team helping your daughter-athlete

A concussion requires that teachers must be part of the process. He lists "brain breaks" to "study buddy" and other items for students, teachers, and parents to appreciate and put into practice.

The entire article and accompanying documents is available at www.training-conditioning.com. In the article's search window, enter: "Upgrading Protocols: Bonus Materials." With the information on the CDC website and from the CAMP program, you can make sure your daughter-athlete is cared for and cleared properly.

Hossler's article (and other concussion programs) is only a reference for athletes and parents. If you are faced with a concussion, this information can guide you through the care from a qualified physician that is required at every level.

Appendix D: The Responsible Use of Social Media

Michael Austin, at www.coachad.com, recently wrote: "Social media has created ways for coaches to notify their players at a moment's notice about upcoming practices, changes in schedules, etc. On the flip side, social media allows players to post their innermost thoughts about your team, your opponents, or even your game strategy online without a filter."

Please make sure your daughter-athlete understands that once she posts to a blog or a website, or sends a text message on a cell phone - it is a permanent record. Always take time to think before you act when posting, texting, or using e-mail.

Many years ago, I thought I had seen the worst posting on one of the first message boards for a respected website. I must admit that between what I see and what I read now; it is now much worse. Pictures and messages today have the potential to cost an athlete much more than a scholarship. It may cost them their opportunity for success now and well into the future.

A college coach or a future employer wants to avoid drama. Drama is draining and counterproductive to a team or an individual's success. Rants on the web are indicative of a high-maintenance individual who is more concerned about herself than her teammates. The old saying still applies: *there is no I in team.*

Austin writes: "Coaches need to have a policy in place for social media use."

The following story needs to be told so everyone is clear about proper social media usage. Many years ago a 15 year old female athlete was verbally abused on a popular message board (how the owner of the site allowed it to be posted still troubles me). The purpose of this message was to take away as much self-confidence from this student-athlete as possible so a teammate could take her place and get more playing time.

The coaches had never seen something like this before and brought in the "suspect." When the student-athlete was questioned, who they thought wrote this post, it became apparent that she did not do it. After bringing in the parents, it was learned that her father posted the message.

The father was not allowed within a three hundred feet of the practice field or a game site. That punishment stopped the posting of rants on a bulletin board message center for that team. The father hired an attorney and the school system dragged it out so that any ruling came after the season ended. Just in case you are wondering, the father lost the ruling at the school district level and never pursued it further.

He did pull his daughter out of the school (against her wishes, per her teammates) and didn't realize that his harmful ways would follow him wherever his daughter played. She was a very good student-athlete and she went to a college 1,500 miles away and gave herself a fresh start. Lucky for her, a college coach did not consider her "baggage" to be detrimental to her future success. Now, in her late twenties, she has a terrific job and is independent and thriving.

However, she has said that period of time took a huge toll on her and the family. As an only child, her father had no other outlet for his fiery spirit and ultimately it led to him getting counseling on how to channel his anger.

I am a realist and I understand how involved adults and relatives can be as I was also the father of a two sport female student-athlete. But, it is still the youngsters who are playing the sports.

Despite what you read in the media or hear from others, not one student-athlete can be officially offered an athletic scholarship until their senior year in high school. There are strict NCAA rules governing contact among coaches, athletes, and parents.

In this day and age of twenty-four hour information flow, be responsible! If you have nothing good to say, keep it to yourself. Youngsters grow up quickly enough now. They do not need drama in their lives; it only endangers their human potential.

Responsible parenting and the lessons learned from sports' participation teaches today's youngsters more than they can imagine. This responsible behavior helps them form a strong foundation so each young lady can become the best she can be on and off of her field of play.

College Coach Dawn Redd writes on her website www.coachdawnwrites.com: "Our athletes have different ways of thinking, different ways that they've been coached, different ways of playing the sport … and different folks who influence their lives. We deal with people from diverse backgrounds and it's our jobs as leaders to mold them into a team."

Recognize that coaches learn where an athlete's head was before recruiting her and she/he has to assess what her potential can be while matriculating at their college. They will help guide a student-athlete to find the right path for her on and off the field of play.

For those parents of youngsters who do not want to play a sport in college; please realize that everything being discussed also applies to the travel ball and high school experiences.

Appendix E: Researchers Conclusions about Females and ACL Injury

MYTH – TRAINERS CAN JUST TRAIN FEMALE ATHLETES SAFELY AND NOT BE UP-TO-DATE ABOUT THE LATEST RESEARCH FINDINGS

Our program has helped adolescent female athletes since 1995 and I am providing a sampling of recent years valued research abstracts highlighting what teen female athletes require during training to minimize their risk for injury.

For too long, many trainers have used male training techniques when training young females. I know that a trainer who has taken advanced training to help female athletes can develop a more effective training program than someone who has not currently studied the unique challenges presented by this population [our CEU program for trainers is offered at www.issaonline.com *Parts 1 and 2; Safely Training the Adolescent Female Athlete*].

The landscape and knowledge about safely training teen female athletes is always changing. It is not enough for a trainer to obtain a degree or become certified and not keep up with the current research. As an example, look at the following abstracts and realize their conclusions form the foundation for safe and age-appropriate training programs for all female athlete training programs.

Previously, I have discussed the kinetic chain and these abstracts are not meant to blow you away with medically based terms; rather they have been included so you gain an appreciation for valued research and the conclusions the researchers have reached.

Look at the bold items and you can read that researchers have pointed the way for the exercises that trainers need to utilize to help all female athletes minimize their risk for injury with BNP Training to stabilize the adolescent female athlete's lower body and helping every young woman so she can become the best student-athlete each can be while having fun playing their sport(s).

Sports Med. 2010 May 1;40(5):367-76. doi: 10.2165/11531340-000000000-00000.

Young women's anterior cruciate ligament injuries: an expanded model and prevention paradigm.

Elliot DL, Goldberg L, Kuehl KS.

Source: Division of Health Promotion & Sports Medicine, Department of Medicine, Oregon Health & Science University, Portland, Oregon 97239-3098, USA. elliotd@ohsu.edu

ABSTRACT
Anterior cruciate ligament (ACL) injuries among young female athletes occur at rates three- to eight-times greater than in male competitors and, in general, females experience more sports injuries than males, when balanced for activity and playing time. ACL injuries are a particular concern, as they result in immediate morbidity, high economic costs and may have long-term adverse effects. While several closely monitored ACL injury preventive

programmes have been effective, those efforts have not been uniformly protective nor have they achieved widespread use. To date, **ACL injury prevention has focused on neuromuscular and anatomical factors without including issues relating more broadly to the athlete. Coincident with greater female sport participation are other influences that may heighten their injury risk. We review those factors, including early single sport specialization, unhealthy dietary behaviours, chronic sleep deprivation and higher levels of fatigue, substance use and abuse, and psychological issues.** We augment existing models of ACL injury with these additional dimensions. The proposed expanded injury model has implications for designing injury prevention programmes. High school athletic teams are natural settings for bonded youth and influential coaches to promote healthy lifestyles, as decisions that result in better athletes also promote healthy lifestyles. As an example of how sport teams could be vehicles to address an expanded injury model, we present an existing evidenced-based sport team-centered health promotion and harm reduction programme for female athletes. **Widening the lens on factors influencing ACL injury expands the prevention paradigm to combine existing training with activities to promote psychological well-being and a healthy lifestyle. If developed and shown to be effective, those programmes might better reduce injuries and, in addition, provide life skills that would benefit young female athletes both on and off the playing field.**
PMID:20433210[PubMed - indexed for MEDLINE]

Am J Sports Med. 2011 Mar 7. [Epub ahead of print]
Timing of Lower Extremity Frontal Plane Motion Differs Between Female and Male Athletes During a Landing Task.

Joseph MF, Rahl M, Sheehan J, Macdougall B, Horn E, Denegar CR, Trojian TH, Anderson JM, Kraemer WJ.

Source: Human Performance Laboratory, Kinesiology Department, University of Connecticut, Storrs, Connecticut.

ABSTRACT
BACKGROUND: **Female athletes are at a greater risk for non-contact anterior cruciate ligament injuries than male athletes**. Gender differences in frontal plane kinematics (hip adduction, knee valgus, and ankle eversion) and temporal relationships that make up the components of dynamic knee valgus may explain this discrepancy.

HYPOTHESIS: The authors hypothesized that women would reach peak frontal plane kinematic values earlier during landing compared with their male counterparts.

STUDY DESIGN: Controlled laboratory study.

METHODS: Hip, knee, and ankle 3-dimensional kinematics were measured using high-speed motion capture in 10 National Collegiate Athletic Association Division I female athletes and 10 male practice squad athletes during a drop-jump landing. Independent t tests were used to analyze each dependent variable to identify differences between genders.

RESULTS: Maximum hip adduction, knee valgus, and ankle eversion occurred earlier in women than in men (mean differences 33.7% of stance [95% CI, 20.2%-47.2%], 41.7% [95% CI, 31.5%-51.6%], 16.5% of stance [95% CI, 7.3%-25.6%], respectively). Maximum hip adduction and knee valgus occurred before maximum knee flexion in women and after in men (mean differences 0.11 seconds [95% CI, 0.05-0.18 seconds], 0.19 seconds [95% CI, 0.13-0.25 seconds], respectively). Maximum ankle eversion occurred earlier in women than in men (mean difference 0.06 seconds [95% CI, 0.01-0.11 seconds]). There was a significant difference between genders for angular velocity of knee valgus (mean difference = 25.53 deg/sec [95% CI, 8.30-42.77 deg/sec]).

CONCLUSION: Frontal plane kinematic temporal relationships at the hip, knee, and ankle differ between genders. The components of dynamic knee valgus peak during the deceleration phase in women and during the acceleration phase in men during a drop-jump landing. These data suggest that men and women employ a completely different kinematic landing/jumping strategy and that women land and collapse very rapidly into valgus compared with their male counterparts.

CLINICAL RELEVANCE: **The differences in timing of the components of dynamic knee valgus between women and men may contribute to the increased risk of noncontact anterior cruciate ligament injuries in female athletes. There may be implications for neuromuscular reeducation training in those at risk for anterior cruciate ligament injury** so the components of dynamic valgus occur later in the landing phase of jumping.
PMID: 21383083 [PubMed - as supplied by publisher]

Br J Sports Med. 2009 Dec;43(14):1100-7. [Epub 2009 Nov 1.]

PREDICTION AND PREVENTION OF MUSCULOSKELETAL INJURY: A PARADIGM SHIFT IN METHODOLOGY.

Quatman CE, Quatman CC, Hewett TE.

The Sports Medicine Biodynamics Center and Human Performance Laboratory, 3333 Burnet Avenue, Cincinnati, OH 45206, USA. carmen.quatman@gmail.com

Traditional methods employed to study musculoskeletal injury mechanisms and joint biomechanics utilise in vivo or in vitro techniques. The advent of new technology and improved methods has also given rise to in silico (computer modelling) techniques. Under the current research paradigm, in vivo, in vitro and in silico methods independently provide information regarding the mechanisms and prevention of musculoskeletal injury. However, individually, each of these methods has multiple, inherent limitations and is likely to provide incomplete answers about multifactorial, complex injury conditions. **The purpose of this treatise is to review current methods used to study, understand, and prevent musculoskeletal injury and to develop new conceptual-methodological frameworks that may help create a paradigm shift in musculoskeletal injury prevention research**. We term the fusion of these three techniques in simulacra amalgama, or simply in sim, meaning a "union of models done on the likeness of phenomena." Anterior cruciate ligament (ACL) injury will be employed as a model example for the utility and applicability of the proposed, synthesised approach. Shifting the current experimental paradigm to incorporate a multifaceted, multidisciplinary, integration of in vivo, in vitro and in silico methods into the proposed in sim approaches **may provide a platform for a more comprehensive understanding of the relationships between complex joint biomechanics and observed injury mechanisms**.
PMID: 19884108 [PubMed - in process]

Arthritis Rheum. 2004 Oct;50(10):3145-52.

High prevalence of knee osteoarthritis, pain, and functional limitations in female soccer players twelve years after anterior cruciate ligament injury.

Lohmander LS, Ostenberg A, Englund M, Roos H.

Source: Lund University, Lund, Sweden.

ABSTRACT
OBJECTIVE:

To determine the prevalence of radiographic knee osteoarthritis (OA) as well as knee-related symptoms and functional limitations in female soccer players 12 years after an anterior cruciate ligament (ACL) injury.

METHODS:

Female soccer players who sustained an ACL injury 12 years earlier were examined with standardized weight-bearing knee radiography and 2 self-administered patient questionnaires, the Knee Injury and Osteoarthritis Outcome Score questionnaire and the Short Form 36-item health survey. Joint space narrowing and osteophytes were graded according to the radiographic atlas of the Osteoarthritis Research Society International. The cutoff value to define radiographic knee OA approximated a Kellgren/Lawrence grade of 2.

RESULTS:

Of the available cohort of 103 female soccer players, 84 (82%) answered the questionnaires and 67 (65%) consented to undergo knee radiography. The mean age at assessment was 31 years (range 26-40 years) and mean body mass index was 23 kg/m2 (range 18-40 kg/m2). Fifty-five women (82%) had radiographic changes in their index knee, and 34 (51%) fulfilled the criterion for radiographic knee OA. **Of the subjects answering the questionnaires, 63 (75%)**

reported having symptoms affecting their knee-related quality of life, and 28 (42%) were considered to have symptomatic radiographic knee OA. Slightly more than 60% of the players had undergone reconstructive surgery of the ACL. Using multivariate analyses, surgical reconstruction was found to have no significant influence on knee symptoms.

CONCLUSION:

A very high prevalence of radiographic knee OA, pain, and functional limitations was observed in young women who sustained an ACL tear during soccer play 12 years earlier. These findings constitute a strong rationale to direct increased efforts toward prevention and better treatment of knee injury.

Copyright 2004 American College of Rheumatology

References and Websites Cited

NOTE FROM AUTHOR
Shakespeare W; Sea change was coined by Shakespeare, in Ariel's song *Full Fathom Five* in The Tempest (1611)
> – http://www.thefreedictionary.com/sea+change

Chapter 2

www.learn2trainsafely.com – BNP Training.

Chapter 3

Vicki Harber, Ph.D. Canadian Sport for Life: *The Female Athlete Perspective*. 2008. And Chapter 12.

For Women in Sports, A.C.L. Injuries Take Toll. Jere´ Longman. Edward Wojtys, M.D. quote, March 26, 2011.

Lohmander LS, Ostenberg A, Englund M, Roos H. *High prevalence of knee osteoarthritis, pain, and functional limitations in female soccer players twelve years after anterior cruciate ligament injury*. Arthritis Rheum., Oct;50(10):3145-52. 2004

James Elliot, M.D., Michael Willis, M.D., Peter Millet, M.D. *Knee injuries in female athletes reaching 'astronomical' levels.* The Billings Gazette website, November 7, 2010.

Chapter 4

Sage GH and Loudermilk S. *The female athlete and role conflict.* APEA Research Quarterly. 50(1): 88-96, March 1979.

Barry CH, Western Michigan University. *Female collegiate gymnasts and experiences in sport retirement due to injury,* UMI Number: 3340181, 2008.

Gilbert and Williamson. *Sport is Unfair to Women.* SI; 38, May 1973:88,

Lance LM. *Gender differences in perceived role conflict among university student-athletes.* The University of North Carolina at Charlotte. 2004.

Preamble to Title IX of the Education Amendments of 1972.

Holliman K. *Consensus statement on female athlete medical issues released by sports medicine groups.* Orthopedics Today, March 2004.

http://www.thefreedictionary.com.

Chapter 5

Hewett T, Ph.D., Noyes F, M.D. *Plyometric training in female athletes.* The American Journal of Sports Medicine.; Vol. 24, Number 6 1996 and Dr. Frank Noyes quote.

Everson D, PT, Matheson J DPT, Wilkins K, DPT. *Decreasing the Incidence of ACL Injuries in Pediatric/Adolescent Patients; Screening Techniques and Program Design.* Gillette Children's Specialty Healthcare. Management of Musculoskeletal Conditions in Children and Adolescents workshop, December 3, 2010.

Ireland M, M.D. *Anterior cruciate ligament injury in female athletes: epidemiology.* J Athl Train, 1999 Apr;34(2):150-4.

Greydanus DE, M.D., Omar H, M.D., Pratt HD, M.D. *The Adolescent Female Athlete: Current Concepts and Conundrums.*, Pediatric Clinic of North America, 57 (2010) page 698 – Table 1.

Wojtys EM, Wylie BB, Huston LJ. *The effects of muscle fatigue on neuromuscular function and anterior tibial translation in healthy knees.* Am J Sports Med. 1996;24:615- 621.

Ireland M, M.D., Leetun D, M.D. *Gender Differences in Core Stability as Measured by Trunk and Hip Performance.* Kentucky Sports Medicine February 2002.

Zebis MK, Ph.D. *EMG Finds "High Risk" Zone for ACL Tears in Female Athletes.* American Journal of Sports Medicine, October 16, 2009.

Groeger M. *Injury Risks for the Female Athlete*; ACSM Health & Fitness Journal July/August, 2010.

Matheson J T, Wilkins K, Everson D. *Decreasing Incidence of ACL Injuries in Pediatric and Adolescent Patients.* Gillette Children's Specialty Healthcare, December 3, 2010.

Chapter 6

Carpenter L J, Ph.D., Acosta V, Ph.D. Brooklyn College. *Women in intercollegiate sport, a longitudinal national study twenty nine year update, 1997-2006*, 2008.

National Women's Law Center. *Keeping Score: Girls' Participation in High School Athletics in Massachusetts*, 2004.

Colton, M. & Gore, S. *Risk, Resiliency, and Resistance: Current Research on Adolescent Girls*. Ms. Foundation for Women, 1991.

Tiggemann, M. *The impact of adolescent girls' life concerns and leisure activities on body dissatisfaction, disordered eating, and self-esteem*. The Journal of Genetic Psychology; 2001.

2005 Graduation-Rates Report for NCAA Division I Schools. NCAA, 2005.

Lopez MH & Moore K. *Participation in Sports and Civic Engagement*. The Center for Information and Research on Civic Learning and Engagement. 2006.

Miller, K, Sabo, D.F., Melnick, M.J., Farrell, M.P. Barnes, G.M. *The Women's Sports Foundation Report: Health Risks and the Teen Athlete*. Women's Sports Foundation. 2000.

Kulig K, Brener N, McManus T. *Sexual activity and substance use among adolescents by category of physical activity plus team sport participation*. Pediatrics and Adolescent Medicine. 2003.

The Women's Sports Foundation Report: Sport and Teen Pregnancy. Women's Sports Foundation. 1998.

Stevenson B, Ph.D.. *Beyond the Classroom: Using Title IX to Measure the Return to High School Sports*. Wharton School of the University of Pennsylvania. 2008.

A report from the Feminist Majority Foundation's Task Force on Women and Girls in Sports. 1995.

Benefits of Physical Activity. A study by Melpomene Institute.

Corneliβen T, Pfeifer C. *The Impact of Participation in Sports on Educational Attainment: New Evidence from Germany*. The Institute for Athletics and Education. Discussion Paper No. 3160. November 2007.

Erickson D, a personal development trainer.
http://www.essortment.com/all/psychologyofsp_rdhl.htm.

5 Reasons for Girls to Play Sports. http://www.kidshealth.org.

The Women's Sports Foundation.
http://www.womenssportsfoundation.org.

Chapter 7

Redd D. *A Navigational Map For Coaching Female Athletes*.
www.coachdawnwrites.com.

Steidinger J, Ph.D. Psychology Today online. February 13, 2011.

Chapter 8

CPT Waterman, BR, M.D., Langston, JR, BS, Cameron, KL, PhD, ATC, LTC Belmont, PJ Jr, M.D., LTC Owens, B D, M.D. LER – online – *Sprain in the Forecast: Epidemiology and risk factors for ankle sprain,* April 2011.

Ireland M M.D. Sports Medicine Update. American Orthopaedic Society for Sports Medicine, 1999.

Reynolds G. *Phys Ed: Preventing ACL Injuries in Girls.* New York Times, September, 2009. And Chapter 10.

Hewett TE, Torg JS, Boden BP. *Video analysis of trunk and knee motion during non-contact anterior cruciate ligament injury in female athletes: lateral trunk and knee abduction motion are combined components of the injury mechanism.* Br J Sports Med. 2009 Jun;43(6):417-22. Epub 2009 Apr 15.

Chapter 9

Lephart SM, Henry T. *The Role of Proprioception and Neuromuscular Control in the Management of Joint Pathology. 1*997 workshop at University of Pittsburgh.

Osternig L, Ph.D., ATC. *The Role of Coactivation and Eccentric Acticity in the ACL-Injured Knee.* Chapter 34. Lephart and Henry 1997 workshop at U of Pittsburgh.

Barrack R, M.D. and Munn B, M.D.. *Effects of Knee Ligament Injury and Reconstruction on Proprioception*. Chapter 19. Lephart and Henry 1997 workshop at U of Pittsburgh.

Lephart SM, Fu FH. *Proprioception and Neuromuscular Control in Joint Stability*. Am J Sports Med. Jan-Feb;25(1), *130-7*, 1997.

LaBella C, M.D. *Warm-ups cut sports injuries in teen girls: study*. Reuters Health article. November 10, 2011.

Mandelbaum BR, Silvers HJ, Watanabe DS, Knarr JF, Thomas SD, Griffin LY, Kirkendall DT, Garrett W Jr. *Effectiveness of a neuromuscular and proprioceptive training program in preventing anterior cruciate ligament injuries in female athletes: 2-year follow-up*. Am J Sports Med. 2005 Jul;33(7):1003-10. Epub 2005 May 11.

Kirkendall, DT. Ph.D.; Garrett, WE Jr, MD., Ph.D. *The Anterior Cruciate Ligament Enigma: Injury Mechanisms and Prevention*; Section I: Symposium: Women's Musculoskeletal Health: Update for the New Millennium. Clinical Orthopaedics & Related Research: March 2000 - Vol 372; 64-68.

Chapter 10

Hirst HE, Ameau E, Parish T. *Recognizing anterior cruciate ligament tears in female athletes: What every primary care practitioner should know*. The Internet Journal of Allied Health Sciences and Practice. Vol. 5, No. 1, Jan 2007.

www.STOPSportsInjuries.org

O'Brien M, M.D., sports medicine physician at Children's Hospital Boston rule

Geier CD Jr M.D., http://www.drdavidgeier.com/about/

Chapter 11

Dolins KR, Ed.D., RD, CSSD, CDN. *In the Dark*. Training and Conditioning, Vol. XX, No. 8, November 2010; pages 25-31. And Chapter 12.

Chapter 12

Power curve. Adapted from International Sports Sciences Association.

Schinfeld JS, M.D., 1995. Advisor to Sport Fit Conditioning Programs™ .

Arja L.T. Uusitalo, M.D., Ph.D.. *Overtraining*. The Physician and Sportsmedicine. Vol. 29, No. 5; May 2001|

Gatorade Sports Science Institute; *Minimizing chronic athletic fatigue among swimmers; special emphasis on nutrition*, 1991; 35(4)

Kimberly J. Templeton, M.D.. *Women's Sports Injuries: It's Not Just The Hormones. March 2007*;

Note: Additional references and definitions are available at www.learn2trainsafely.com

Additional Resources – Reading and Websites

READING

Communication differences between male and female team sport athletes by Philip Sullivan

Games Girls Play: Understanding and Guiding Young Female Athletes by Caroline Silby PhD and Shelley Smith

Gender and Competition: How Men and Women Approach Work and Play Differently by Kathy DeBoer

Sports Her Way: Motivating Girls to Start and Stay with Sports by Susan M. Wilson

The New Toughness Training for Sports: Mental Emotional Physical Conditioning by James E. Loehr and Chris Evert

Warrior Girls: Protecting Our Daughters Against the Injury Epidemic in Women's Sports by Michael Y. Sokolove

WEBSITES

Canadian Sport for Life; http://canadiansportforlife.ca/blog/young-female-athlete-dr-vicki-harber

Coach Dawn Redd; http://coachdawnwrites.com/

LEARN2TRAINSAFELY.COM; http://www.learn2trainsafely.com

Legislative history of Title IX: http://www.now.org/issues/title_ix/history.html

Tucker Center at the University of Minnesota; http://www.cehd.umn.edu/tuckercenter/

Report: Developing Physically Active Girls (http://www.cehd.umn.edu/tuckercenter/projects/tcrr/default.html)...not

Women's Sports Foundation; http://www.womenssportsfoundation.org/

Index

AAOS – See STOP sports injuries 107

ACL [anterior cruciate ligament] and injury ii, 3, 8, 13 – 18, 25, 33
    – 35, 38 – 40, 66, 68 – 70, 80, 82, 84 – 85, 93 – 101, 119, 139,
    147 – 152, 152 – 154, 157, 160
        See osteoarthritis (OA) and ACL injury 13 – 15, 40,
            79, 96, 153, 155

ACSM Health & Fitness Journal 157

Activities of daily living [ADL] 110, 118

Advanced training 120

Agility 114, 117, 125 – 126

American College of Sports Medicine [ACSM] 25, 45

American Journal of Sports Medicine 156, 157

A navigational map for coaching... - See Redd D 47 – 63, 159

Amenorrhea [loss of monthly cycle] 33, 139

Anorexia nervosa 109

Ankle sprain risk factors 67

Assessment 2, 37, 73, 94, 117, 141, 153

Athlete training gains made 6, 30, 81, 121, 126

Athleticism 21 – 22, 83, 121

BNP training 8 – 9, 24, 39, 67 – 68, 71, 73, 79, 81 – 83, 100, 115,
    117, 148, 155

Balance 4, 8, 12, 19, 36, 38 – 40, 68 – 69, 71, 73, 76, 81, 110, 118,
    141

Benefits of female sports participation 41 – 45

Binge-eating disorders 109

Biomechanics 9, 17, 71, 75 – 76, 128, 152
Blue Shoes – See Rider J, Ph.D. 131
Building a foundation training program 117
Bulimia 109
Burnout – See Overtraining 107, 122 – 124

Canadian Sports for Life 11
Cardiovascular endurance 43, 75
Certification courses – volunteer coaches 84 – 85
Challenges for female athletes 8, 13, 16, 24, 31, 33, 36 – 39, 63, 72, 74, 79, 80, 93 – 95, 97, 104, 113, 127, 139, 147
        at puberty 31, 139
Coaching today's female athlete 47 – 64
    Coach Dawn Redd 47, 60, 145, 162
Concussions 77, 141 – 142
Consensus statement 2004 25 – 26, 156
Core training – See Training 39, 66, 73
Cross training 22, 24, 74, 76, 81, 90 – 91
Cutting 8, 68 – 69, 71, 75, 76, 119

Depth jumping 119
Disordered eating 109 – 110, 158
Dolins K, Ed.D., RD, CSSD, CDN 109
        In the Dark article excerpts 109 – 111, 122

Eating disorders 33, 41, 109, 133, 139
Elliott J, M.D. 17, 155
Ernst, Bob – quote i

Faster 24, 35, 39, 65, 71, 84, 131
        Faster, quicker... 24, 39, 71, 84, 109
Female athlete challenges

Female athlete triad 12, 33, 96, 109, 139

Females are not males with less testosterone i, 36

Field of play ii, 39, 64, 94, 99, 118, 125, 127, 145 – 146, 175

Filer, R, PT, CSCS 5, 27, 98, 100

Flexibility 32, 38, 114, 117, 125

Foundation training – See BNP Training 115, 117

Fun and female athletes 2, 22, 25, 44, 59, 74, 76, 86, 98, 101, 104,
        107 – 108, 110, 127, 129, 148

Functional joint stability 95

Functional training 12

Geier CD Jr., M.D. 108, 162

Gillette Children's Specialty Healthcare 33, 139, 157

Goals iii, 7, 9, 23, 55, 57 – 62, 64, 66, 90, 98, 103 – 104, 106, 108,
        110, 118, 136

Go low, Go slow 118

Gordon S, Ph.D. 5 – 7

Greydanus, M.D. and teen female athlete challenges 38, 157

Hard and smart training iii, 27, 102

Harber V, Ph.D. 11, 121, 155, 163

Hewett T, Ph.D. 34, 36, 40, 70 – 71, 84, 96, 128, 151, 156, 160

Hossler P – concussion 141 – 142

Injured teen female athletes interviews 100 – 107

Integrated sports training 125

Interval training 72, 119 – 120, 126

        Submaximal training 119, 123

Ireland M, M.D. 35, 39 -40, 68, 70, 157, 160

ISSA [International Sports Sciences Association] 28, 177

        CEU courses; Potash, et al 28, 84, 147, 177

Jumping 8, 34, 47, 68, 71, 75 – 76, 83, 119, 121, 139, 151
      Landing 34, 69, 71, 76, 119, 1 3 9, 149 – 151
Lower body 24, 35, 36, 39, 66, 71, 79, 82, 95, 115, 148
      Training 71, 79
      Stabilization 15

Key reasons why females need to train to play sports 36, 173
Kinetic chain 39, 115, 148

Knee 17, 34, 38 – 39, 75, 96, 115, 155
      Tracking 36, 71

LaBella C, M.D. 83 – 84, 161
Learn, train, perform 93
Lephart S, et al 81 – 82, 95, 160 – 161
Life skills training 2, 45, 54, 62, 76, 103, 149
Ligaments – See ACL and PCL 13, 34, 65, 96, 116, 117, 140
Listening to female athletes 26

Mandelbaum B, M.D. – See PEP Program 84, 161
Matheson JT 40
Mechanoreceptor function 82
Medical history 2, 37, 72, 75, 94, 116 – 117
Minimize risk of injury 36, 39, 71, 85, 97, 99 – 100, 107, 113, 117, 127, 129, 147 – 148, 175
Motor development 17
Muscle memory 22 – 24, 76, 79
Musculoskeletal injury 151 – 152
Myths
      Females do not need to train differently than males 16
      My daughter-athlete will get an athletic scholarship 28
      It costs a lot of money to train 71

Every trainer can train a teen female athlete 94

Disordered eating is not a major issue 109

My daughter-athlete will not get hurt 113

Trainers can just train female athletes safely… 147

Neuromuscular control 8, 36, 39, 67, 73, 81, 116, 118, 160

Neuromuscular training ii – iii, 11, 24, 68, 76, 127 – 128

Next hurdle for teen female athletes 2, 39,129

Nutrition for daily energy 64, 109

No downside to safe and age-appropriate training 3, 35

Non-contact ACL injury ii, 15, 35, 40, 66, 69, 85, 97

      Public health challenge – See Wojtys quotes 13, 16
         – 17

Noyes F, M.D. 34, 36, 70, 156

Nutrition 75 – 76, 109 – 111, 122 – 123, 125 – 126, 128, 162

      Guidelines 135 – 138

O'Brien M, M.D. – 3 S rule 108, 162

Osteoarthritis |OA| 13 15, 40, 79, 96, 153, 155

Osteoporosis 33, 43, 45, 111, 139

Overhead |overhand| athletes 23, 96

Overtraining – See Burnout 80, 107, 122 – 124, 162

PCL |posterior cruciate ligament| 8, 13, 104 – 105

PEP Program – See Mandelbaum 84

Perceived exertion |PE| 120

Periodization planning 80, 94 – 95, 122 – 124

Plyometrics 72, 156

Position of no return 35, 40, 68 – 69, 71

Postural stability 67 – 68

Potash W – quote i, 6, 36

Power 8, 27, 30, 36, 39, 44, 51, 55, 59, 61, 70, 84, 114 – 117, 126
       Power formula 114, 162
Proprioception 8, 36, 39, 67, 73, 76, 81 – 82, 84, 118, 160 – 161

ROM [range of motion] 102, 114, 116 – 117, 126
Redd D 47, 159, 163
Reps [repetition] 118 – 120
Rider J, Ph.D. – *Blue Shoes*; Afterword 131 – 134
Run 25, 38, 74

Safe and age-appropriate training 3, 13, 27 – 28, 35, 37, 39, 72, 81,
    94, 97, 113 – 115, 118, 125, 147
Shoot for the moon – quote 104
"Silent epidemic" 13, 97
Social media use 143 – 146
Speed 4, 6, 66, 114, 117, 125, 126
Sports challenges for teen female athletes 95, 97
Sports participation – females iii, 6, 13, 15, 20, 26, 32, 35, 41 – 43,
    62, 76 – 77, 97, 103, 108, 119, 127, 145
          See Life skills training
STOP sports injuries (AAOS) 107
Steidinger J, Ph.D. 60 – 62, 160
Stevenson B, Dr. 42, 159
Stretching 66, 72, 74 – 76, 115, 117, 120
Strength training 6, 36, 40, 43, 66 – 72, 75, 91, 103, 111, 114 – 118,
    120 – 121, 125 – 126
Student-athlete iii, 7, 26, 29 – 30, 85, 95, 100, 104, 106, 118, 127 –
    128, 144 – 145, 148, 175
Submaximal – See interval training 119, 123
Successful conditioning program 74

Teen female athlete changes at puberty 33, 39

Templeton K, M.D. 128, 162

Title IX 19 – 21, 26, 38, 41, 131 – 134, 156, 159, 164

Training to play sports iii, 3, 7, 13, 17, 18, 23, 25, 27, 37, 39, 65, 80 – 81, 97, 128 – 129, 175

    Sport-specific training 8 -9, 12, 43, 75, 118, 125 – 126, 141

    Translates onto field of play 94, 117, 121

Uusitalo A, M.D., Ph.D. 123, 162

Value training to play sports 3, 7, 18, 25, 33, 97, 129

Volunteer youth coaches 1 – 3, 7, 24, 73, 84 – 85, 121

Warm-up 72 – 74, 81, 83 – 84, 120, 161

Waterman BR, CPT, M.D. 68, 160

Willis M, M.D. 18, 155

Wojtys E, M.D. [Voy ■ tus] 13, 15, 16 – 17, 25 – 26, 38, 85, 155, 157

Women's Sports Foundation 42, 45, 158 – 159, 162 – 164

For those who want a FREE synopsis of how to help your adolescent female athlete; "Contact Us" at www.learn2trainsafely.com and request the Key Reasons and Training Tips.

Use Code: **KeyR12**

Our daughters want to play a sport(s) and we, as parents, are very excited to support their hopes and dreams – even more so if you were an athlete, as I was. More than likely, you start out in a community youth sports organization and do what you are told to do. You never stop to think: Maybe my coach does not really know what is best for my daughter?

Please understand – I do not believe there is something nefarious going on – some way of thinking that purposely is stressing skills training over my, and other healthcare professionals, concept of "training to play sports."

Rather, the topics covered in this book have not become part of the mainstream dialogue. Another hope of mine is that all adults will realize there is a better, and a cost effective, way to minimize the risk for injury for all female athletes. In recent years, researchers are stating that 9 -12 year old females need training to play sports.

I am certain that my program will work for any age group; but I caution you that **my primary goal is to help all adolescent female athletes by helping each female student-athlete become the best athlete she can be on and off her field of play**.

– Warren J. Potash

Place order for BNP Training
www.learn2trainsafely.com

Enter Code
and receive free download
Code: **TNB-11-134**

5 Simple Steps to Ensure You
Choose a Quality Conditioning/Training Program
That Will Produce Results for You

CONTACT US at www.learn2trainsafely.com

Code: **STEPS-5**

You will receive a FREE guide by e-mail

➤ Go to www.learn2trainsafely.com for more information and for ordering the **BNP Training Program**.

Coaches – if you are ordering for all of your athletes, please go to "Contact Us" and let us know the quantity required and we will provide a quote to make your purchase the most cost effective for all of your athletes.

➤ ISSA website for trainers to earn CEU credits – *Safely Training the Adolescent Female Athlete;*
www.issaonline.com

Made in the USA
Middletown, DE
20 March 2017